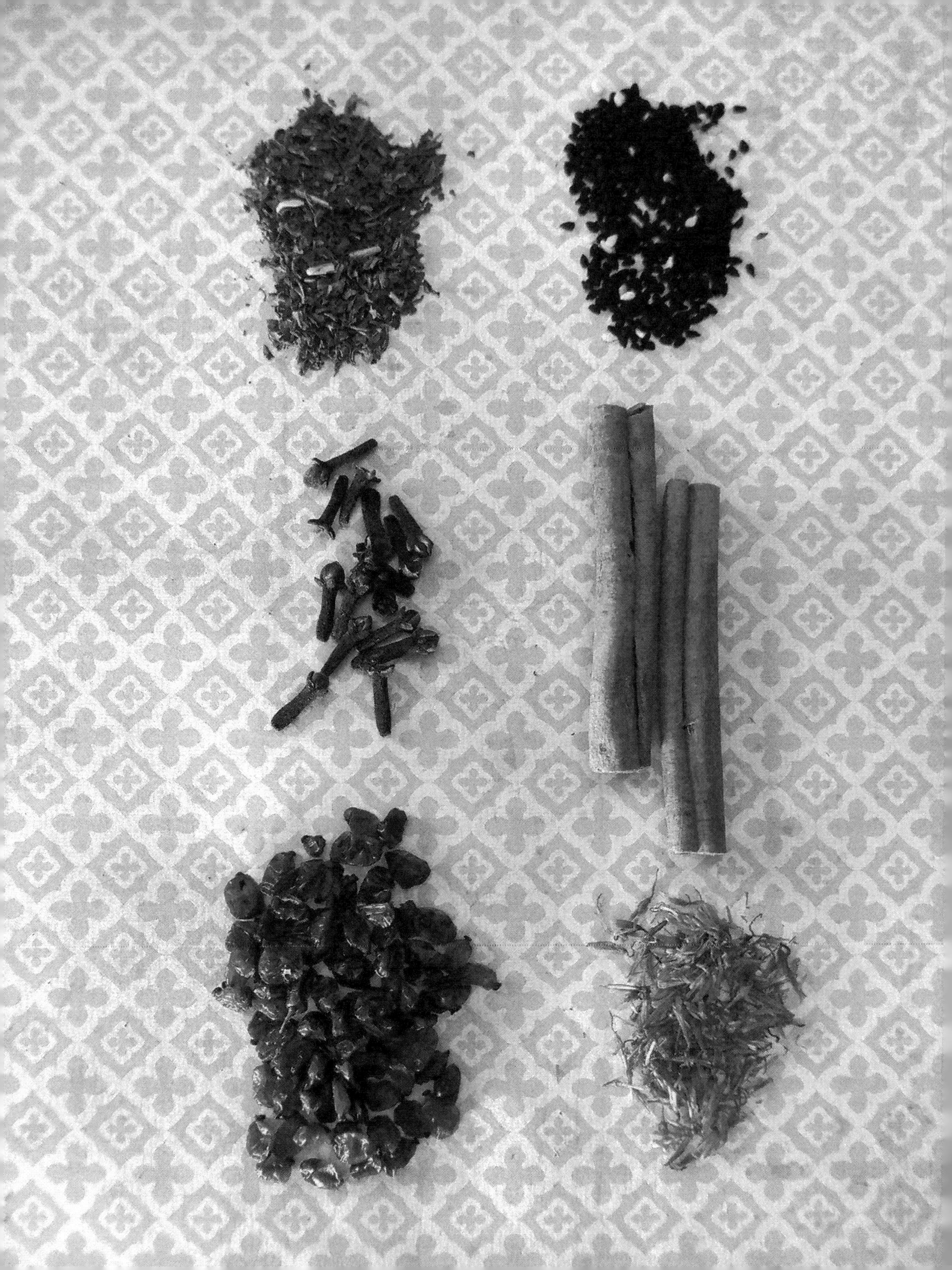

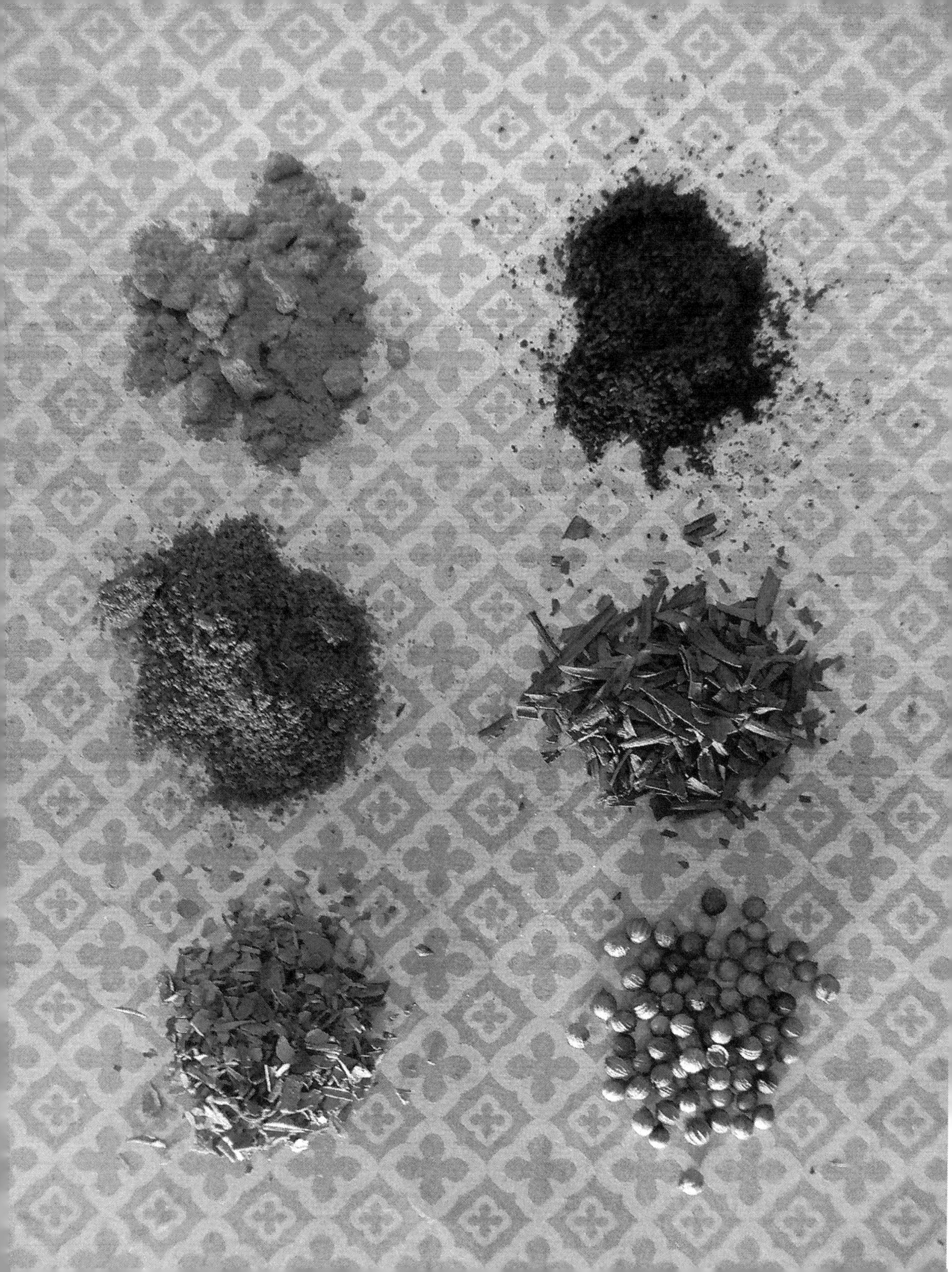

Everyday Persian

Everyday Persian

Your Essential Guide to the Modern Iranian-

American Kitchen

Written and published by Tina Rezvani

Copyright © 2015 Tina Rezvani

All rights reserved.

This book or any portion thereof may not be reproduced or used in any manner whatsoever without the express written permission of the publisher except for the use of brief excerpts in a book review or article. Permission may be requested by contacting rezvanipublishing@gmail.com.

Interior photography by Tina Rezvani.

Cover design by Sarah Hutto: www.saraholiviadesigns.com

First Printing, 2015

ISBN-13: 978-1508463160

ISBN-10: 1508463166

To Mom, Dad, and Masoud

"Stay close to anything that makes you glad you are alive."

— Hafez, 14th-century Persian lyric poet

Contents

Preface: Persian or Iranian?	1
Introduction	2
The Cuisine in Context	10
Inside a Persian Pantry: Important Ingredients	16
Useful Kitchen Tools	38
Cooking Techniques	42
Dining Etiquette	48
Notes on Using This Book	51
Breakfast	54
Salads	69
Soups	81
Egg Entrees (*Kuku*)	97
Stew Entrees (*Khoresht*)	108
From the Grill: Kabobs & More	123
Additional Entrees	138
Rice	159
Sides and Snacks	182
Pickles	202
Desserts	209
Beverages	227
Index	239
About the Author	249

Preface: Persian or Iranian?

In 1935 the nation of Persia's name was officially changed to Iran. In today's political context it is therefore more accurate to use the term 'Iranian' when discussing the country and its people. However, in a cultural context, many Iranians use both 'Persian' and 'Iranian'—sometimes interchangeably—to describe themselves.

There are numerous reasons why so many continue to identify as Persian. Most commonly, people use it to identify with the Persian ethnic group as there are several other ethnic groups living in Iran. Some use it to distance themselves from the Islamic Republic and connect with a deeper, centuries-long cultural history dating back to the Persian Empire. Others simply prefer the way it sounds. To avoid any confusion, throughout this book I use 'Iranian' when referring to the country and its people and 'Persian' when referring to food and other aspects of culture.

Introduction

Welcome (khosh amadid)! Let's drink some tea and discuss our love for Persian food. Oh, you're unfamiliar with it? Not to worry—this book is here to help.

My journey in writing this book began in 2009, when I began researching and writing a master's thesis on the cultural significance of traditional dinner parties (*mehmooni*) for Iranians living in the United States. I was in graduate school studying cultural anthropology, a fitting subject for me since I love learning about the world and its people, places and experiences. I observed that the *mehmooni* are some of the most culturally rich experiences I've had while growing up as a second-generation Iranian-American, even if participants don't necessarily think of them that way. Stories and memories are shared over food, music and dance; conversation topics range from poetry and jokes to family, friends, work and politics. Iranians rarely shy away from discussing politics and other such serious matters at the dinner party table; rather, it seems that a deep political and social consciousness is always running through our veins, perhaps owing to

Iran's tumultuous history and the stressful circumstances that many have experienced: revolution, war, and the upheaval of social norms.

My father was born in Kashan, a city located south of Tehran in Iran's Isfahan Province. Historically, Kashan was a large center for the production of beautiful ceramic tiles and pottery. The Persian word for tile, *kashi,* refers back to this city. These stunning tiles feature the vivid blues and yellows and intricate geometric patterns the world has come to associate with Islamic architecture. My mom is from Tehran, Iran's capital and cosmopolitan center. My parents always made sure to buy and prepare fresh food whenever possible for our family. Thanks to them, I didn't grow up eating much processed or frozen food since our kitchen was always stocked with the ingredients needed for a fresh meal.

Iran is a beautiful place that is rich with history, culture, art, natural diversity, kind and hospitable people, and delicious food. I've visited Tehran three times and have many fond memories of the city. Walking along its streets, you'll find vendors selling everything from fresh fruit juices to succulent grilled meats. Persian bazaars are truly a feast for the senses, with vendors selling heaping mounds of colorful spices, nuts and dried fruits. Most people in Iran still buy freshly baked bread each morning from their local bakery. Supermarkets are small and located on neighborhood street corners, with piles of fresh fruit displayed outside. Everywhere, there's an intriguing blend of the old with the new.

Contrast the bustling city streets with the peaceful interior of someone's home at dinner. In general, it is within people's homes that you'll find the very best Persian cuisine. I like to think of Persian cooking as slow-cooked comfort. Home cooking is still the norm in Iran, but there's also a long and proud tradition of street food, a robust industry within a culture that embraces going out and being seen. Everywhere in Tehran, you can see friends and family walking, picnicking and socializing together outdoors. In contrast, while restaurant culture is a relatively recent phenomenon, Iranians—particularly the younger generation—have quickly embraced it along with many other global influences. Iran is a young country, with nearly 70 percent of its population being under 35 years old. This generation craves connections with the rest of the world. In Iran, especially in Tehran, you can dine on everything from hamburgers and fried chicken to pizza and Chinese food.

In Persian culture, hospitality is critically important. There's an old Persian saying that describes a guest as a gift sent from God. Good hospitality is also crucial for maintaining a strong reputation. Such hospitality begins in the home and means that anyone who enters will be treated respectfully and offered tea, or perhaps a cold fruity drink in the summer, or a delicious meal (or maybe all three!). It means that no one who comes over for dinner will leave before they're stuffed to the brim.

Food is highly important in social relations and the Iranian-American experience. I don't feel particularly aware of my ethnicity on a daily basis, and I don't imagine that others do either. Like your eye color, it's not something you think about all the time. But whenever I am in a grocery store buying some yogurt, eggplants or pomegranates, I feel a connection.

Growing up, I savored the evenings when my parents would prepare a large Persian feast before having guests over. In the hours before these parties, large pots of aromatic Persian stews would simmer on the stovetop along with even larger large pots of fragrant basmati rice. Perhaps some saffron-infused fish or poultry would be contributing its own wonderful aroma from within the oven. All sorts of delicious treats would be laid out on the living room table. Fruit is significant in Persian culture and cuisine, and most Iranians will leave out a fruit bowl all the time, especially at dinner parties. Guests arrive, tea is poured, and food, music and conversation (and maybe even dancing) ensue into the late hours of the night.

If you've ever been a dinner guest at an Iranian's house, you may have been surprised at the sheer volume of food that is prepared. This goes back to hospitality—it is always better to go above and beyond in providing for your guests than to not have enough. It is both an act of kindness and the passing down of a tradition (plus, who can resist having delicious leftovers for days?).

Eating has become a central part of the way I relate to my heritage as it has for people around the world. I am mostly a self-taught cook and have learned what I know from experimenting in the kitchen, reading recipes and watching cooking shows. I distinctly remember being around six years old and sitting in our dining room with a wooden spoon and a large pot of water with a few radishes floating around in it. I loved to stir the radishes around and around the pot and pretend that I was cooking up a feast. (Thankfully, my culinary skills have progressed since then!) From pho to falafel, I absolutely love to eat, but I also find cooking to be a powerful way to release creative energy.

"Food is our common ground, a universal experience."

– James Beard, champion of American cooking

My training in cultural anthropology inspires me to seek out the threads that tie us together as humans. As a strong dimension of cultural identity, food has had the power to unite us for nearly our entire existence on this planet. And that makes sense—after all, we all need to eat. Sharing a meal is, perhaps, one of our most fundamentally human activities and one of the most fun ways that we bond with each other. As omnivorous novelty-seekers, we are always on the lookout for new and exciting taste experiences. Exploring the food of another culture is part adventure, part desire to connect with others in an authentic way. Trying the foods of different cultures is like inviting each other into our lives. Bite by bite, we can come closer to mutual understanding.

Maybe you've just tried Persian food for the first time and are dying for more. Maybe you have a Persian spouse, significant other, or friend and want to cook for them—or maybe you are Persian but never learned to make the meals you grew up eating. You've come to the right place! This book is meant to be more than just a collection of Persian recipes. It is designed to teach you the basic ingredients and structure behind Persian cooking so that once you've mastered the recipes, you will be able to go further and experiment with ingredients to create your own Persian-inspired dishes.

This book is *not* meant to be an exhaustive catalog of nearly every traditional Persian dish out there. I've included many of the most popular dishes as well as my personal favorites. However, beyond those I've also included several recipes that have been influenced by my experience as an Iranian-American. I cook what I like to eat, and my cooking reflects my experience of growing up as the child of immigrants. I like to skirt the border between cultural sharing and an authentic culinary heritage. Call it "fusion" cuisine or not, but mixing elements of different culinary traditions is probably my favorite way of cooking. It comes naturally when, like me, you have grown up eating between two cultures.

The experience of growing up as the child of immigrants is familiar to millions. If it isn't familiar to you, then the main point I would convey is that it gives one the sense of constantly living between two worlds—you're not quite one thing, but not quite the other. How do I ensure that I have something tangible to share to reflect the Persian part of my identity? I believe the sharing of food, and the preservation of the tradition of Persian hospitality, may be the most accessible way.

I hope you enjoy this culinary adventure and discover some new favorite meals. As we say in Farsi, *nush-e-jan* (our version of *bon appetit,* roughly translating to "nourishment of life!")!

The Cuisine in Context

"If more of us valued food and cheer and song above hoarded gold, it would be a merrier world."

— J. R. R. Tolkien, *The Hobbit*

Colorful, complex and often unexpected, Persian food perfectly reflects its nation of origin. From dusty bazaars stacked with intricate carpets to lush green forests along the Caspian Sea; from rosewater distilleries to centuries-old mosques; from the arid central desert to the luxury ski resorts north of Tehran, it takes time to truly understand Iran, its diverse people and its complex history. But, no matter where you go, there's always spectacular food.

Persian cuisine is as colorful and visually inviting as it is delicious, from platters of fragrant saffron rice served at dinner parties to tart, juicy pomegranates for dessert. Throughout centuries, this ancient and versatile cuisine has seen a myriad of influences. Located in the heart of the Middle East, Iran is one of the region's largest countries, spanning an area slightly smaller than Alaska. It is a diverse country that is home to several ethnic groups, languages and religions.

Civilization in Iran is ancient, estimated by historians to date back to 6,000 BCE. Over the centuries, Iran's borders have shifted often as empires expanded and contracted, and as a result, Persian cuisine has seen many influences. Persia once reigned over a vast empire spanning from modern-day Egypt to India, and was subsequently invaded by the Greeks, Mongols, Ottomans and Arabs. Not only did these groups bring with them their own customs and foods, but they exported much of what they found in Iran back to their home countries. Iran's location between Europe and Asia served Silk Road traders and explorers well; these travelers helped spread ingredients like saffron, pistachios and pomegranates far and wide. In later centuries, Great Britain, Imperial Russia and France also left footprints behind through their colonial ventures within the country.

Within the nation's borders lies a rich natural bounty. Iran's fertile farmlands are abundant with saffron, pistachios, walnuts, tea, plums, cherries, peaches, apricots, watermelons, wheat, rice, barley, and a variety of other crops. As a result, Persian cooking emphasizes working with fresh, seasonal ingredients, and it incorporates a rich array of fruits, herbs, legumes, nuts, spices and grains. These key ingredients are enhanced with the addition of spices like sumac and turmeric.

In the United States, we are fortunate to have such a diverse population and access to all types of cuisine. Many nationalities have a longer history of immigration to the U.S. than Iranians, who didn't start coming to the U.S. in significant numbers until the 1970s, and therefore they've had more time to introduce their styles of cooking. If you are unfamiliar with Persian cuisine, you are not alone. In general, it remains relatively little-known within the United States, although it is more familiar in regions with larger Iranian populations (like California). While Persian food shares similarities with Mediterranean, Turkish and Indian cuisine, it is distinct. Today, recipes vary regionally depending on local culinary traditions and available ingredients. For example, Iranians in the north or the south, near the Caspian Sea or the Persian Gulf, eat more fish. And you're more likely to find hot and spicy dishes in the southern region of Iran, where people in the port cities had more contact with those from India and other regions where spicy food is prevalent.

Key Flavors

The beauty of preparing different cuisines lies in how it can expand your knowledge of the uses of familiar ingredients. Persian food is known for unexpected combinations (for example, the inclusion of fruit in almost anything. Try chicken stew with peaches, an omelet with dates, or *torshi miveh*—pickled fruit—and you will never go back to thinking of fruits in the same way).

In my view, the most prominent flavors in Persian dishes fall into four categories: tart, sweet, herbal and rich. The best Persian cooking combines some or all of these flavors to produce a balanced dish. Some of the common ingredients for each flavor include the following:

Tart	Lime, tomato, yogurt, sumac, pomegranate, sour cherry, barberry, pickles, verjuice
Sweet	Fruit, dried fruit, honey, sugar, saffron, cardamom, cinnamon, rosewater
Herbal	Parsley, fenugreek, chives, onions, scallions, cilantro, mint, basil, tarragon, turmeric, cumin, garlic, shallots, radishes
Rich	Meat, eggs, rice, nuts, butter, beans, eggplant

'Hot' and 'Cold' Foods

"Let food be thy medicine and medicine be thy food."

— Hippocrates, ancient Greek physician

Traditional Persian nutrition follows an old system, believed to have originated with ancient Chinese medicinal practices, that categorizes different foods as being 'hot' or 'cold' depending not on their temperatures but on the effects they have on the body. Eating too much hot food or too much cold food is believed to cause an imbalance (*sardi* or *garmi*, coldness or warmth) that can lead to illness. Therefore, the heating and cooling properties of different foods were traditionally taken into consideration when developing recipes. The idea is to create balance while emphasizing foods that complement your body's own nature, which can also be hot or cold. This knowledge has been passed down through generations, and some combinations have become common knowledge (for example, yogurt and watermelon are both considered cold, so eating too much of them together would be avoided).

Setting Up a Persian Meal

Traditionally, Persian meals were served upon a *sofreh*, or large tablecloth, laid out on the floor. The dishes would be arranged on top of the cloth, and families would sit on the floor around the *sofreh* and share their meal. This tradition still lives on (especially in rural areas of Iran), but for the most part, families eat around tables now.

Persian meals don't consist of 'courses' such as appetizers and entrées. A meal consists of a variety of dishes that are served at the same time and are meant to be eaten together. These might include one or two entrées, rice and/or bread, a platter of herbs and accompaniments, yogurt, salad and pickled vegetables (*torshi*). Therefore, Persian cooking has evolved over time to produce flavors that complement each other when eaten together. A *khoresht* with rice may taste great on its own, but I guarantee that the flavors will only get better when they intermingle with sides of yogurt, herbs and *torshi*. The ubiquitous bed of fluffy Persian rice becomes like a canvas soaking up all of these flavors.

Inside a Persian Pantry: Important Ingredients

Most of the ingredients that you'll need in order to prepare Persian food are readily available in the average U.S. supermarket. This section lists more specialized ingredients as well as others that really define Persian cooking. You can search for specialty ingredients at Persian, Middle Eastern and international grocery stores—and, of course, practically everything is available online. Some good websites include:

Sadaf	www.sadaf.com
Golchin	www.ofdusa.com
Kalamala	www.kalamala.com
Amazon	www.amazon.com

Meat and Poultry

Lamb – Lamb refers to the meat of a young sheep less than two years of age. The meat of mature sheep is referred to as mutton and has a stronger flavor and tougher texture than lamb. Choose meat that is lighter in color, as this indicates younger lamb (which is tenderer). Lamb has an aromatic flavor that pairs well with almost anything but goes especially nicely with fruits, herbs and spices.

Poultry – The ever-versatile chicken is as ubiquitous on Persian dinner plates as it is on American ones. At one time in history, duck was commonly eaten in Iran, but for reasons unknown its popularity has faded over time while turkey has increased in popularity.

Beef – From ground beef to tenderloin fillet, beef is used extensively throughout Persian cuisine. If you're limiting your consumption of red meat, then you can substitute poultry, beans or vegetables in almost all recipes as needed.

Offal – Kabobs made from offal, or organ meats (including liver, heart, and kidneys), are traditionally eaten in Iran. Braised beef tongue, eaten with rice or made into sandwiches, is also popular, and it's absolutely delicious. In addition, a hearty breakfast soup called *kaleh pacheh* made with a lamb's head and hooves, flavored with cinnamon and lemon, is a traditional food still enjoyed by many.

Fish – In Iran, several varieties of fish are caught in the Persian Gulf, Caspian Sea, and the country's rivers and streams. A mild, firm-fleshed white fish is best for most Persian recipes. Salmon also works very well in certain dishes such as *sabzi polow-mahi* (fish with herb rice), a traditional meal for Nowruz (Persian New Year). I always encourage choosing only sustainably-caught seafood. The Monterey Bay Aquarium Seafood Watch is a great starting point for learning about sustainable options: www.seafoodwatch.org

~*~*~

Dairy

Yogurt – Plain yogurt is ubiquitous in a Persian kitchen. It is on the table during almost every meal, and it is used in side dishes, marinades, rice and even soups. You can use either regular or strained or Greek-style yogurt.

Cheese – The most popular type is a fresh cow, sheep or goat cheese that is similar to—but somewhat milder in flavor than— Greek feta. Persian and Middle Eastern grocery stores generally carry a variety of fresh cheeses packed in water. Compared to the popularity of yogurt, the use of cheese is light throughout traditional Persian cooking. It is most often eaten with warm bread (a combination called *nan o panir*) for breakfast or as a light meal.

Kashk – This is a rich, creamy fermented whey product that adds a tangy yet savory depth of flavor to recipes (think liquid Parmesan cheese). It can also be used as a thickening agent or a garnish. *Kashk* is sold in both liquid and dried forms. I recommend liquid, but dried works too—you just need to reconstitute the dry *kashk* with hot water. It is readily available online and in Middle Eastern grocery stores, but if you're in a pinch, you can usually substitute sour cream.

~*~*~

Starches and Grains

Rice – A staple of Persian cuisine. For authenticity, long or extra-long grain rice such as basmati rice is the best option. While white rice is traditional, brown basmati is also available. I really like the nutty flavor and chewy texture of brown rice and enjoy its use in Persian recipes.

Bread – In Iran, people still buy fresh bread every morning from their neighborhood *noonvah* (bread baker). I absolutely love this ritual, as there is nothing quite as comforting and satisfying as freshly baked bread, no matter where you are.

There are four main varieties of traditional Persian bread: *lavash*, *barbari*, *sangak* and *taftoon*. All are flatbreads and are baked in traditional clay ovens. Here, you can buy them at Persian grocery stores and bakeries (and sometimes even online). Since they are typically sold in very large, flat, sheet-like loaves, the most convenient thing to do after you take them home is to immediately slice them into individual portions, then bag and freeze what you won't use that day. For the best texture and flavor, reheat these breads in an oven or toaster.

Lavash is a very thin and flexible bread, similar to a flour tortilla, which is ideal for making sandwich wraps. *Barbari* is an oblong bread, about 1 inch thick, with vertical ridges. *Sangak* and *taftoon* are medium thickness and slightly chewy. *Sangak* is usually shaped like an elongated triangle and sprinkled with sesame and/or nigella seeds. Its name comes from *sang*, meaning 'stone,' due to the fact that it is baked in the oven on a bed of scorching hot stones. *Taftoon* is baked into large, flat rounds.

Wheat – Aside from its use in breads, wheat is also consumed in other forms. Pelted or bulgur wheat is the basis of a breakfast porridge called *haleem*. Germinated wheat is made into a sweet paste called *samanu* and eaten as a New Year's dessert.

Barley – I love the chewy texture of cooked barley and use it most often in soups. Wheat and barley have been grown in Iran since the onset of agricultural practices. Cultivation of barley dates back to Neolithic times in the Fertile Crescent.

~*~*~

Nuts and Seeds

Pistachios – Pistachios are undeniably the most important nuts in Persian cuisine. Aside from being a tasty snack, they are also used in desserts and rice dishes. Iran is the leading worldwide producer of pistachios. If you can find Iranian pistachios, use them, as they will taste more authentic. There is a marked taste difference between these and California pistachios due to the former's higher meat content, higher levels of unsaturated fat, and higher roasting temperature.

Walnuts – Walnuts are a popular accompaniment to bread, cheese and herbs (*nan o panir o sabzi*), are turned into sauces, and in Iran they are even sold as a snack by street vendors.

Almonds – Crunchy, delicious almonds are eaten as snacks with various spices and seasonings. They are also frequently used in desserts, stews and rice dishes.

Nigella seeds – These small, black seeds of the species *Nigella sativa* have a flavor similar to onions and cumin and are often sprinkled on breads, cheeses and pickled vegetables. You can find them sold as nigella seeds or in Indian markets as *kalonji*. They are also sometimes labeled as onion seeds or black cumin.

Seeds – In most Persian kitchens you will find *ajil*, a popular "trail mix" consisting of dried fruits, nuts and seeds. Seeds of all kinds are popular snacks, especially pumpkin and sunflower. Even watermelon seeds can be roasted and enjoyed by the handful.

~*~*~

Beans and Legumes

Lentils – High in protein, lentils are an easy and healthy ingredient to incorporate into your cooking routine. They vary in color and size. Persian cooking generally uses green or brown lentils. In preparation for Nowruz, Iranians sprout lentils to create bouquets of bright green "lentil grass" (*sabzeh*) to display on the traditional Nowruz *sofreh* (table spread); the sprouts represent rebirth.

Yellow split peas – Usually found dried, these peas are added to various stews and meatball recipes. When properly cooked, the peas are not mushy but retain a slight bite to them. To avoid overcooking, you can parboil them separately and add them to your dish during the later stages of cooking.

Mung beans – The common white bean sprouts that you toss in stir fries and salads are made from mung beans. These small, dark green beans have a sweet flavor and are added to Persian stews and rice. Like lentils and split peas, mung beans do not need to be soaked prior to using.

Fava or broad beans – These have a sweet, fresh flavor and are mixed with rice and herbs or eaten alone as a snack similar to edamame. If you can't find fresh fava beans, many stores carry frozen ones. Lima beans can be used as a substitute in recipes that call for fava beans.

Chickpeas (garbanzo beans) – These dimpled beige legumes were among the earliest to be cultivated. They are very versatile, have a sweet and nutty flavor, and can be used in whole form or dried and ground into chickpea flour (*aard-e nokhodchi*).

~*~*~

Fruits

Pomegranates – The pomegranate is native to Persia, and the fruit, which symbolized fertility, is a common motif in Persian art. Buy fresh pomegranates in season (fall and winter). The seeds, called arils, can be extracted and frozen for up to three months. When selecting a pomegranate, choose a fruit that is dark to pinkish red, heavy, firm, and without cracks or blemishes. The best pomegranates will have arils that are juicy, plump, and ruby-like.

Persimmons – These delicious fruits look similar to orange tomatoes but have a very sweet, almost floral flavor. They should only be eaten when ripe. Choose persimmons that are deep orange in color (it is okay if there are some black spots on the skin), plump, and slightly soft, depending on the variety (Fuyu persimmons remain firm even when ripe, while Hachiya persimmons will soften).

Cucumbers – Because of their cooling properties, cucumbers are very popular during the summer months. Most Iranians I know eat cucumbers like apples—as a snack anytime and anywhere. For snacking, I recommend the variety labeled "Persian cucumbers"—they are smaller and thinner but have few seeds and a nice crunch.

Dates – Dates have a rich, dense texture and a complex sweet flavor that make them my go-to replacement for chocolate when the latter is unavailable. When possible, choose plump Medjool dates for the best texture and flavor. They should be soft, moist and have a "melt in your mouth" quality. If Medjool aren't available, get any dates that are whole. The pre-chopped ones (which are usually dusted with sugar or chemicals to reduce stickiness) lose a lot of their great flavor and texture.

Watermelon – The old Iranian trick for choosing a watermelon is to rap on it with your knuckles and listen. It is ripe if it makes a hollow sound. Watermelons are revered for their ability to quickly hydrate and cool you down. Sliced watermelon is ubiquitous on a summertime dessert table alongside ice cream and cake.

Sour cherries – Also called tart cherries or morello cherries, these are the sour cousins to regular sweet cherries. In Iran, they are highly popular dried, juiced, made into jams, preserves and fruit leather, mixed with rice, and used to flavor desserts. In the U.S., fresh tart cherries are harvested in July but can be difficult to find unless you live in one of its growing regions (Michigan, New York, Pennsylvania, Wisconsin, Washington and Utah are tart cherry-producing states). You are more likely to find them frozen, canned, jarred or juiced. Persian and Middle Eastern grocery stores usually carry tart cherry products.

White mulberries – Native to northern China, these berries have a very mild, lightly sweet flavor. Their leaves are used to feed silkworms. In Iran, they are eaten both fresh and dried. It's not easy to find fresh white mulberries in the U.S., but the dried ones are readily available in Persian grocery stores and online.

Barberries – These tart little red berries grow on shrubs throughout Europe, North Africa, and the Middle East. Dried barberries are easily found in Persian grocery stores, but if you need a quick substitute you can use cranberries. They are traditionally used in rice, poultry and egg dishes, but they are very versatile and can be also added to salads, breads and pastries. Barberry juice is also sold by street vendors in Iran during the hotter months.

Quince – Quince is in the same family as apples and pears. Due to its high pectin content, quince makes great jams and preserves, and in fact, that is the most popular form it takes in Persian cuisine. Although the raw fruit is firm and tart, it makes a deliciously sweet jam. Quince jam is one of the most popular types of jam in Iran.

Green plums – Known as *gojeh sabz* (green tomato) in Farsi, these crisp, green, unripe plums are usually eaten with a sprinkle of salt. The combination of crisp, sour and salty is simply mouthwatering! *Gojeh sabz* can be found at many Persian supermarkets when they're in season (generally late spring). They are quite addictive, so if you find them, I recommend buying a lot!

Citrus fruits – Citrus fruits are used extensively throughout Persian cuisine, especially limes. Look for those marked as Persian limes, which have thin skins.

~*~*~

Vegetables

Onions – The aroma of frying onions is a familiar one in a Persian kitchen. Caramelized onions form the base of nearly every Persian dish. Raw onion is also mixed with ground beef, used to marinate and tenderize meat, pickled, and even eaten plain alongside a meal. For most recipes, yellow Spanish onions work just fine. I like to use red onions in salads for their color.

Eggplants – For everyday cooking, choose large purple (globe) eggplants or Italian eggplants (similar to globe but smaller). Baby eggplants (or Indian eggplants) are only a few inches long and are used for pickling. Eggplants have a mild enough flavor that they can be easily manipulated to fit within different dishes. In fact, I've heard the eggplant referred to as the "Persian potato" due to its popularity.

Shallots – The Persian shallot (scientific name *Allium stipitatum*), called *musir*, is a different species than the kind you see in most supermarkets. Persian shallots have a garlicky flavor as opposed to the oniony flavor of regular shallots. Dried Persian shallots are available online and in Persian grocery stores and can be soaked and rehydrated prior to using.

Grape leaves – Often stuffed and baked into *dolmeh*, these delicate, dark green leaves are usually brined and sold in jars at Middle Eastern and Mediterranean grocery stores.

Radishes – Spicy and crunchy, radishes are usually eaten raw alongside a meal for added flavor or sliced and eaten with bread, butter, cheese and herbs.

Spinach – The word 'spinach' actually originates from its Farsi name *esfenaj*, and it is thought that spinach was first cultivated in Persia.

Squash – Whether zucchini, pumpkin or yellow squash, squash is commonly used in many stews and meat dishes, and its seeds are a popular snack.

Carrots – Many Persian dishes magnify the natural sweetness of carrots, from julienned carrots mixed with barberries and rice to chicken stew with carrots and dried plums. When I was a kid my grandmother would make sweet, sticky carrot jam whenever she came to visit us since she knew how much I liked it. It might sound strange, but it is actually delicious!

Potatoes – In French, the potato is known as *pomme de terre,* or "apple of the earth." In Farsi, this is also true; *sib-e-zamini* also means "apple of the earth." Potatoes made their way around the world from South America, and today they are used in all kinds of Persian dishes, because who can resist this down-to-earth yet delicious tuber?

~*~*~

Herbs

The use of herbs, both fresh and dried, is widespread throughout Persian cooking. Fresh herbs are also eaten with bread and cheese for breakfast or a light meal and alongside many dishes as *sabzi khordan* ('eating herbs'). Fresh herbs were the original salads of Persian cuisine. Salads, as we know them today, were introduced to Iran by other cultures.

Parsley, dill, tarragon, mint, basil, chives, cilantro, and **oregano** are some herbs you will want to keep on hand, either fresh or dried. I recommend always keeping dried versions of these in your pantry or freezer. The good news is that if you keep an herb garden and are wondering how to use up all of its bounty, cooking Persian food is a great way to do so!

Herbs that may be less familiar include:

Fenugreek – Long used for its medicinal properties, fenugreek adds a sweet, somewhat nutty flavor to dishes. Fenugreek goes very well with vegetables and beans. Be careful, though, because a little bit goes a long way, and using more than a small amount will actually produce a bitter taste. Fresh fenugreek can be somewhat difficult to find. Indian grocery stores and international farmer's markets are the best places to check. Persian grocery stores carry dried fenugreek leaves, and you might also be able to find powdered fenugreek seed in the spice section of your local farmer's market. For most Persian recipes, dried fenugreek leaves will suffice.

Borage – Dried purple borage flowers, called *gol gav zaban* ('cow's tongue flower'), are brewed into a hot tea with added lemon and/or sugar. The tea is used to calm the nervous system and aid in fighting colds and coughs.

~*~*~

Spices and Seasonings

Turmeric – Native to India, turmeric powder is a warm, earthy, bright yellow spice made from ground turmeric root, a member of the ginger family. Turmeric is also what gives yellow mustard its vibrant color (and be careful, it can stain your clothes and countertops!). Like fenugreek, a little bit goes a long way since using too much in a recipe can produce a bitter, metallic taste.

Saffron – Famously the most expensive spice in the world, saffron is obtained from the dried stigmas of the small purple crocus flower and is sold in delicate threads. Iran produces a large volume of saffron, and the spice is very prevalent throughout Persian cooking, from chicken to rice to desserts. The threads are usually ground into a powder which is brewed in hot water (I call this "saffron water" throughout the book), as opposed to being added directly to a dish.

Sumac – Sumac is one of my very favorite seasonings. It is a tart, lemony spice made from the ground, unripe berries of the sumac bush. It is most commonly sprinkled on beef kabobs, but it is also delicious on lamb, fish, shrimp, rice, and in marinades and salad dressings.

Cardamom – The green variety of this uniquely fragrant spice is used to flavor desserts and tea as well as rice and stews. Black cardamom has a stronger, smokier flavor. You can buy cardamom either already ground or as whole seed pods. For the best flavor, it is best to get the pods and remove and grind their seeds yourself. Green cardamom has a taste that is slightly sweet, slightly citrusy, and slightly anise, and it is excellent in tea and coffee, desserts and pastries, as well as a variety of savory dishes.

Coriander seeds – These are dried cilantro seeds and have a bright herbal flavor. They can be ground into powder or used whole.

Dried rose petals – Roses are widely consumed in the form of rosewater, jam, or dried petals. The petals are crushed or ground and used to flavor and garnish dishes.

Dried limes – Known as *limoo amani*, these are added to dishes to impart a sour flavor. They are available either whole or ground. Dried limes are made by boiling Persian limes in salt water and then drying them out in the sun. The limes turn very dark brown on the outside and inside, and they become hard. If you're using whole dried limes, soak them in hot water first and then pierce them with a fork before adding them to your dish to help release the most flavor. When cooked, dried limes are wholly edible. You can also buy them ground into a powder called *gard-e limoo* (lime powder), which can be substituted for the whole limes. Fresh lime juice can usually be substituted for dried lime (in a ratio of 1 tablespoon juice to 1 whole dried lime), but the dried limes impart a slightly earthy flavor in addition to the sourness that is lacking in fresh juice.

Golpar – This highly aromatic spice comes from the seeds of the flowering plant known as Persian hogweed (*Heracleum persicum*), which grows wild throughout the mountainous regions of Iran. You can find it in Persian grocery stores labeled "angelica seed," although this is technically not the correct name. The seeds are often powdered and used as a seasoning, especially for beans and legumes, potatoes, pickles, and pomegranate seeds.

Advieh – *Advieh* means 'spices' in Farsi, but it also refers to a spice blend that you can use to season dishes, similar to the Indian *garam masala*. The specific mixture varies by region and cook, but it usually contains any of the following ingredients: turmeric, cumin, cinnamon, cardamom, ginger, nutmeg, cloves, rose petals, sesame, *golpar* powder and black pepper. You can buy it premade at a Persian grocery store or experiment to create your own blend.

~*~*~

Pantry Items

Cooking fats – For most Persian cooking, you should use a mild-tasting fat that can stand up to high heat without burning.

In my recipes I have mostly used canola oil, but you can use whatever oil you prefer. Animal fat, coconut oil, butter and clarified butter (known as ghee, which has a higher smoke point than butter) are also good options. Olive oil is a great choice for dressings, garnishes and marinades but not for high heat cooking since it burns easily and can become toxic.

Tea – Enjoying a hot cup of *chai* anytime—whether it's after a meal or in the middle of a hearty outdoor hike—is a quintessential Persian ritual. Hot black tea brewed from quality loose tea leaves is the national beverage of choice.

Tomato paste – Tomato paste is used as a secret weapon to add depth of flavor to many Persian dishes. It's one of those must-have ingredients that every cook should keep in their pantry.

Pomegranate syrup – Also known as pomegranate molasses or pomegranate concentrate, this thick syrup is used in dishes that call for a sweet-and-sour balance.

Rosewater – Rosewater is used to impart a delicate floral flavor to desserts and beverages. The process of making rosewater by distilling rose petals was first developed in Persia. If you ever have the opportunity to visit a rosewater distillery, go—you won't soon forget that amazing fragrance!

Pickles – Called *torshi,* pickled vegetables and fruits are believed to aid in digestion. Iranians traditionally eat small amounts of *torshi* with meals, similar to Korean *kimchi* and Indian pickles and chutneys. Try putting *torshi* on sandwiches and burgers for a delicious burst of flavor.

Tamarind – Tamarind is a bean-like fruit with seeds that are encased in brown pods. The seeds are surrounded by pulpy dark orange flesh which has an amazing sour, fruity flavor. This pulp can be eaten right out of the pod, and it is also extracted and sold as a paste and a concentrate. The pulp, eaten like candy, is a popular snack in Iran. Tamarind concentrate is easy to use for cooking and is available in Indian, Asian and Persian grocery stores. Tamarind is used primarily to flavor meat and fish stews in southern Iranian cooking.

Useful Kitchen Tools

It's likely that you already own most of the equipment that you'll need to prepare Persian meals. There's no need to buy anything fancy, but there are certain essential tools that *will* make your life a lot easier! These are listed and described below.

Large pot for cooking rice. Rice grains nearly double or even triple in size when they're done. You want to make sure your pot is large enough so that the boiling water doesn't spill over the sides and create a sticky mess on your stovetop. A tight-fitting lid and a thick, heavy bottom are crucial features for a rice pot. A heavy bottom will ensure more even heat distribution and prevent the rice from burning easily.

Colander with fine holes for washing and draining rice. Persian rice preparation follows several steps, including washing, parboiling, draining and steaming the rice. Without a proper container in which to drain and rinse the rice, the process can become less efficient. Make sure the holes of your colander are small enough to prevent rice from falling through.

Kitchen towel or cloth lid cover to place between the pot and its lid while the rice steams. The fabric absorbs moisture and prevents condensation from dripping back into the rice, helping to create perfectly fluffy grains of rice.

Large pot or Dutch oven for cooking stew entrées (*khoresht*). Choose a sturdy, heavy-bottomed pot or Dutch oven with a tight-fitting lid.

Frying pan/skillet for caramelizing onions and making *kabob maytabeh* (pan-fried kabobs) and meat patties.

Sauté pan for sautéing vegetables and other ingredients.

Slow cooker for making *khoresht* and *aash* (thick soup). Because stews and braises are so popular in Persian cooking, a slow cooker can be a very handy device to have, especially if you are hoping to reduce the time you spend in the kitchen.

Food processor for pureeing and chopping onions, nuts, herbs, and other ingredients.

Kabob swords/skewers for preparing all types of grilled meat kabobs. These are long metal skewers with flat blades. Bamboo skewers will not work for most Persian kabobs as they are too small and thin. Metal skewers also have the advantage of heating up and helping to cook the meat from within during grilling.

Basting brush for brushing marinade on kabobs during grilling.

Handheld straw fan to fan and help build up the flames of a charcoal grill before grilling kabobs. This is a traditional tool that can be replaced with whatever you have on hand as a good fanning implement (folded up newspaper works too!).

Mixing bowls for combining ingredients.

Sharp knives for slicing and chopping.

Teapot and kettle for tea preparation. An **infuser** is optional, and a **strainer** will also help keep tea leaves out of cups. A **samovar** was traditionally used to prepare tea but has largely been replaced with more modern tools.

Glass tea cups with saucers for serving tea. Glass allows you to see and adjust the color/strength of the tea.

Casserole or other deep baking dish for baking stuffed vegetables and other meals.

Baking pan or cookie sheet for what else...baking!

Roasting pan for roasting fish, chicken, lamb, etc.

Box grater for grating onions, potatoes, carrots and other ingredients.

Mortar and pestle (or **electric spice and coffee mill**) for grinding saffron threads and whole spices.

Paring knife for peeling fruits.

Citrus zester for forming strips of lemon, lime and orange peels.

Large serving dishes, including platters and trays, for serving meals to guests. It is customary to serve food buffet-style at Iranian parties, and everyone serves themselves.

Rice servers or other flat servers such as a lasagna server or metal spatula.

Serving spoons for serving *khoresht* and yogurt dishes.

Cooking Techniques

Persian cooking uses fairly straightforward methods, but it's always good to know beforehand what lies ahead for you in your kitchen adventures. Here are the most common techniques you'll be using.

Braising – Braised stews of meat, vegetables, herbs, fruits and/or beans are known are *khoresht* and are some of the most common everyday Persian meals. In general, braising refers to the act of searing the food over relatively high heat and then adding liquid (water or stock), covering the food, and cooking it at a lower temperature until the ingredients are cooked through. This method of cooking produces incredibly flavorful results, as all of the ingredients intermingle and the added liquid becomes a sauce.

Caramelizing Onions – *Piaz dagh* (literally 'hot onions') provides the base for nearly all types of *khoresht*. They are also used to garnish soups and dips. These little golden flavor-bombs are so popular that ready-made packages of caramelized onions are available at Persian grocery stores.

To prepare: Peel a large yellow onion and cut off the stem and root ends. Slice the onion in half; then, thinly slice each of the halves. In a large, heavy-bottomed pan, heat about 2 tablespoons of oil or clarified butter over medium-high heat. Add the onion and fry, stirring every 5 minutes or so, until the pieces turn a rich caramel brown. Monitor the pan and make sure you don't burn the onion. Patience is crucial, as it can take around 20 minutes or so for the onion to caramelize completely. Remove the pieces from the oil with a skimmer and drain them on a paper towel.

For convenience, you can fry onions in larger batches and freeze them in gallon-sized storage bags for later use.

Grilling – The smell of kabobs cooking on the grill is pure heaven. Grilling over charcoal is the traditional method, but you can use a gas grill too. Preheat your grill until the surface is very hot (you should only be able to tolerate holding your hand over the surface for a few seconds). During grilling, it's important to turn the kabobs over frequently to ensure even cooking.

Making Tea for a Group – Bring a kettle full of water to a boil. Put four tablespoons of loose tea leaves in a large teapot. Fill the teapot with hot water from the kettle and fill the kettle back up with water. Bring the water to a boil. Remove the kettle's lid and place the teapot right on top of the kettle so that the base of the teapot rests securely in the kettle's opening. Reduce heat to low. The tea leaves will steep in the water inside the teapot and form a tea 'concentrate' that will stay warm on top of the kettle. When you're ready to serve the tea, pour a small amount of the concentrated tea into a glass teacup (filling up about a fourth of the teacup) and top it off with hot water from the kettle. You can adjust the amount of concentrated tea you use depending on how strong you like your tea.

Marinating – The love Iranians have for tart and tangy foods is evident in marinades, which include ingredients like lemon, lime, yogurt, and pomegranate syrup. Grated onions are another key ingredient in meat marinades; not only do they add great flavor, but onions are a natural meat tenderizer. Combine meat and marinade inside a glass, stainless steel or food-grade plastic dish or bag (do not use other metals as they will react with the acids in the marinade). Cover and refrigerate until using. For best results, fish can be marinated for up to one hour, beef for up to one day, and chicken for up to two days.

Pan Frying – Use a solid, heavy frying pan and a small amount of cooking fat. Many Persian foods are pan fried, from *kabob maytabeh* (pan kabobs) and *kotlet* (meat and potato patties) to eggplant. Most of the time, pan fried foods can instead be baked to reduce the amount of fat.

Parboiling – Persian rice is made through a process whereby the rice is rinsed and soaked in water; then it is parboiled (partially boiled), drained, and steamed. The rice is parboiled until it is soft on the outside but retains a firm bite to the inside. See the chapter on rice for more detailed instructions.

Preparing Dried Beans, Legumes and Pulses – Dried lentils, peas and mung beans do not need to be pre-soaked, and they cook relatively quickly. However, most other dried beans do need to be soaked and take longer to cook. First, rinse the beans with water. Then, sort the beans by spreading them out on a towel or pan and picking out any stones or broken pieces. Put them in a bowl and pour in enough water to cover them by 2 inches. Set the beans aside and let them soak for 8 hours or overnight. When they're ready to use, drain them and put them in a large pot. Again, cover them with 2 inches of water, and bring it to a boil. Skim off any foam that develops on the water's surface. Reduce the heat, cover and simmer until the beans are tender and easily mashed with a fork (anywhere from 1-3 hours). Alternatively, you can cook the beans in a slow cooker or a pressure cooker after soaking them.

Saffron Water – Saffron is notoriously expensive, so it's best to make a small amount go a long way. Making saffron water is a way of stretching the amount of saffron needed in a recipe. Grind ¼ teaspoon saffron threads into powder using a mortar and pestle or a spice mill. You can add a pinch of sugar to help grind it more easily. In a small cup or bowl, add the powdered saffron and 1 tablespoon of hot water.

Let the saffron steep in the hot water for about 10 minutes. The water will turn bright red and become infused with a strong saffron flavor. Add the required amount of saffron water to your recipe. You can make this in larger amounts at a ratio of ¼ teaspoon ground saffron threads to 1 tablespoon of hot water. Pour saffron water into a clean glass container and store it in the refrigerator. You can also keep ground saffron threads handy in an airtight container for quick use later.

Salting Eggplant to Extract Bitterness – Eggplant can sometimes taste slightly bitter. To remove the bitterness, slice the eggplant and sprinkle the slices generously with salt. Let them sit for half an hour. The salt will draw out the bitter liquid from inside the eggplant. Rinse and dry the eggplant slices before cooking.

Seeding a Pomegranate – Pomegranates are full of juicy red seeds (called arils) that can easily burst and cause a mess in your kitchen or on your clothes. The arils are encased within the fruit between papery white membranes. There are many methods of removing the arils from the membranes while keeping them intact. Here is one:

Using a sharp knife, make a shallow cut all around the center of the fruit, cutting just through the skin. Grab each half of the fruit and pull/twist it apart to break the pomegranate in half (it's best to do this over a large bowl, which will catch any stray arils that fall when you break the fruit in half). Take one half and gently loosen it by pulling the edges outward, away from the seeds. You should hear it crackle a bit as the seeds loosen. Then hold the half, seed side down, over a large bowl and use a heavy wooden or metal spoon to firmly whack the top until all of the seeds fall into the bowl. You might need to loosen any stubborn arils with your fingers. Repeat with the second half.

Soaking Nuts – Walnuts and almonds are often soaked in salted water overnight. You can do this with pretty much any nut or seed. Soaking makes them easier to digest and creates a lighter and crisper texture. Soaked walnuts are often eaten as snacks or served with bread, cheese and herbs.

Dining Etiquette

Taarof

Here's a common scene between Iranians: One person offers something to another (for example, tea); the second person refuses it, and the first person keeps on offering it to them multiple times, growing increasingly pleading with each offer. The second person refuses multiple times until finally accepting. This back-and-forth refers to a cultural practice called *taarof*, which means "to offer." The idea works in two ways: first, the person doing the offering wants to seem as generous as possible, and the person accepting doesn't want to appear too greedy by accepting too soon. So don't get annoyed when your host keeps insisting that you take what is being offered—if you really don't want it, just keep declining as politely as possible, and thank him or her for her efforts.

Other Tips

- It is generally considered rude to sit with your back turned to someone, so try to avoid this if possible. (Of course, in some situations, you might have no choice.)

- Don't be surprised to see an argument break out over who pays the bill at a restaurant. Iranian hospitality means that one party will do anything possible to prevent the other from paying.

- I like to joke that we run on 'Persian time'. Unless the host has told you otherwise, it is generally better to arrive 20-30 minutes late than to arrive right at the stated time.

- Host/hostess gifts are appreciated. Good options include dessert, wine, an object (like a vase or dish), and flowers.

- A kiss on both cheeks is a common way of greeting friends and family among both women and men.

- At more traditional parties, dinner is usually served late (often around 9:00 or 10:00 p.m.), but there are usually plenty of appetizers to graze on before the main meal.

- Meals are usually served buffet-style so that guests can serve themselves.

A Few Useful Phrases

Merci (MER-see) – *Thank you* (informal)

Khaylee mamnoon (KHAY-lee mam-NOON) – *Thank you very much* (formal)

Khahesh mikonam (kha-HESH MEE-ko-nam) – *You're welcome*

Dast-e shoma dard nakon-e (DAST-eh sho-MAH dard NA-ko-neh) – *May your hand not hurt* (essentially a way of thanking someone for their efforts)

Notes on Using This Book

The recipes within this book fall into two categories:

- Traditional recipes that I have grown up with, inspired by the cooking of family and friends. (Note: These recipes will have their Farsi names listed beside them.)
- Non-traditional or fusion recipes featuring classic Persian ingredients.

Feel free to adjust the recipes to suit your tastes. With the exception of rice and *tahdig*, Persian cooking is rarely about precision engineering—it's more about painting with flavors. Every family has their own recipe and their own way of preparing a dish. If you don't like a certain ingredient, leave it out. If you really love something, feel free to add more than the recipe calls for. If you have dietary restrictions, then make the necessary substitutions.

Herbs are used a lot in Persian cooking. You can usually use fresh herbs and dried herbs interchangeably, unless the quantity of herbs required is large. For example, there is no way to make *ghormeh sabzi*, a spinach and herb stew, using dried parsley and cilantro when you need to use an entire bunch of each. If you don't have fresh herbs on hand, use your judgment when deciding whether to substitute dried (or vice versa).

Several recipes require something I call 'saffron water'. This refers to ground saffron threads steeped in hot water. See the Cooking Techniques chapter for instructions on how to make this. Saffron is expensive, but it is also a defining flavor in Persian food, so use it when you can.

To my vegetarian readers: Many people think of kabobs, shake their heads, and conclude that it's impossible to eat a vegetarian Persian diet. Nothing could be further from the truth! Persian cooking isn't about meat. In most Persian dishes, the meat can be omitted and/or substituted with beans or legumes.

Finally, take advantage of technology like slow cookers, pressure cookers and freezers to increase convenience in the kitchen. Our grandmothers and great-grandmothers had more time during the day to devote to cooking. While it's true that many Persian dishes take some time to prepare well, we don't have to sacrifice a delicious home-cooked Persian meal for our modern-day schedules.

Disclaimer: This book makes reference to traditional beliefs about medicinal properties of various foods. Please note that these statements have not been evaluated by any medical professionals and simply describe beliefs. I make no claims about the efficacy of these ingredients.

Breakfast

~*~*~

A Traditional Breakfast Spread (Miz-e Sobhaneh)

Oats with Sweet Cinnamon Ground Turkey (Haleem)

Eggs on Spinach (Nargesi)

Paisley Fruit Tart

Lentil and Egg Breakfast Burritos

Pomegranate-Nut Granola

Cardamom-Orange Pancakes with Rose Syrup

Eggs Benedict with Persian-Spiced Turkey Sausage, Lavash and Caramelized Onions

Eggplant and Tofu Scramble

Fig, Honey and Cream Cheese Toasts

A Traditional Breakfast Spread (*Miz-e Sobhaneh*)

A basic breakfast usually consists of a *sofreh*, or table spread, that can include several of the following ingredients. The beauty of the breakfast *sofreh* lies in the multiple ways to combine the ingredients. For example, you could have bread with cheese and herbs, or bread with butter and honey, or bread with butter and eggs, etc. It never gets old! The comforting ritual of sipping hot tea and wrapping a piece of warm flatbread around a morsel of creamy feta cheese is one of my happiest food-related experiences. This is my favorite breakfast.

- Hot tea
- Warm Persian flatbread
- Butter
- Cheese
- Sweet cream
- Jam/preserves (popular types include quince, sour cherry, fig and marmalade)
- Honey
- Eggs (usually boiled or fried)
- Sliced tomatoes
- Sliced cucumbers
- Fresh herbs
- Walnut halves
- Fruit

Oats with Sweet Cinnamon Ground Turkey (*Haleem*)

A warm bowl of *haleem* is a treat on chilly mornings. Traditionally, this is a porridge made with pelted wheat. Pelted wheat can be purchased from Persian markets and online. If you can't find it, you can make a much quicker version of *haleem* using bulgur wheat or even plain oatmeal instead, as I have done here. I chose to use ground turkey in this recipe for convenience, but *haleem* can also be prepared with shredded turkey or lamb meat.

4 servings

Topping:
¼ cup unsalted butter
½ pound ground turkey
¼ cup brown sugar
¾ teaspoon ground cinnamon
½ teaspoon salt
Water

If using rolled oats:
4 cups oats
8 cups water, milk or a combination

If using steel-cut oats:
4 cups oats
12 cups water, milk or a combination

- In a large sauté pan, melt the butter and add the turkey. Cook over medium-high heat until the turkey is cooked through, about 10 minutes. While the turkey cooks, use a wooden spoon to break it up into tiny crumbles. Add brown sugar, cinnamon and salt and stir well. Cook for another 2-3 minutes, then remove from heat and set aside.

For rolled oats:

- Add oats and water (or milk) to a pot.
- Over medium-low heat, bring the oats and water to a simmer.
- Stir and cook until the oats soften and the mixture becomes thick.

For steel-cut oats:
- Add the water (or milk) to a pot and bring it to a boil.
- Add the oats and reduce heat to a simmer.
- Cook the oats, stirring occasionally, for 20-30 minutes until they are soft. Add more water and/or milk as needed.

To serve:

- Ladle oatmeal into bowls and top each with the turkey mixture. Serve hot.

Eggs on Spinach (*Nargesi*)

Nargesi comes from the Farsi word for the narcissus flower, *narges*, which has white petals and a yellow center. The eggs in this dish resemble the flower sitting atop a bed of green "grass" (spinach). Infused with the flavors of garlic and turmeric, this is a great alternative to a traditional spinach omelet and is quick and easy to make. Try it as the centerpiece of your next brunch menu.

4-6 servings

1 tablespoon olive oil
1 shallot, minced
1 garlic clove, minced
1 (10-ounce) package frozen chopped spinach, thawed
½ teaspoon ground turmeric
4-6 eggs
Salt and pepper to taste

- In a large pan, heat the olive oil over medium heat. Add the shallot and garlic and sauté until shallot turns golden. Add the turmeric and stir.
- Add thawed spinach and cook, stirring often, for 5-7 minutes until thoroughly heated through. With a spatula or wooden spoon, flatten the spinach in the pan.
- Crack each egg open over the bed of spinach. Cover the pan with a lid and cook until the eggs have reached your desired level of doneness (in my opinion, *nargesi* is best when the yolks are still a bit runny). Season with salt and pepper to taste.
- Cut into pieces and serve with warm bread.

Paisley Fruit Tart

The paisley, or *boteh jegheh*, is a design with Persian origins that is still very popular in textiles and works of art. This gorgeous tart is perfect as a light breakfast or healthy dessert.

6-8 servings

Crust:
1 stick unsalted butter, melted
3 tablespoons granulated sugar
1 teaspoon vanilla extract
¼ teaspoon salt
1 ¼ cups all-purpose flour, plus 2 teaspoons

Filling:
½ cup Greek yogurt (plain or your favorite flavor)
¼ cup honey (optional)

Fruit topping:
Various fruits of your choice (I used berries, bananas and peaches)

Garnish:
Whipped cream
Crushed rose petals

- In a large bowl, whisk together butter, sugar, vanilla and salt. Add 1 ¼ cups flour and mix until a smooth dough forms.
- Sprinkle the remaining flour across a flat work surface. Roll out the dough to a ⅛-inch thick rectangular sheet. Pick it up gently and lay it on a cookie sheet.
- Using the tip of a sharp knife, cut out a paisley shape using as much of the dough as possible. Cover it with plastic wrap and chill it in the refrigerator for 30 minutes.
- Preheat oven to 350°F.
- Remove the dough from the refrigerator. Prick it in several places with a fork, and then bake it in the oven, on the center rack, until golden brown (about 20-25 minutes).
- Remove the crust from the oven and let it cool completely.

- Mix the yogurt and honey together and spread it on top of the cooled crust.
- Cut and arrange fruits of your choice on top of the filling to form a paisley-like design.
- If desired, add dollops of whipped cream and a sprinkle of crushed rose petals. Serve with tea or coffee.

Lentil and Egg Breakfast Burritos

To me, the burrito allows for infinite creativity. There are countless ways you could turn Persian foods into a burrito. This just happens to be one of them, based on my love of pairing leftover lentil rice with scrambled eggs for a quick dinner.

2 servings

1 teaspoon olive oil or unsalted butter
2 eggs
2 large flour tortillas
1 cup Lentil Rice (see recipe on page 170)
½ cup crumbled feta cheese
¼ cup chopped cilantro

- In a pan, heat oil or butter over medium heat. Add eggs and scramble. Remove from heat.
- Arrange tortillas on two separate plates and put half of the eggs, as well as half of the other ingredients, on each.
- Roll in the sides and top of each burrito and serve.

Pomegranate-Nut Granola

I find most commercially available granolas to be too sweet, so in this recipe I have balanced the sweetness of traditional granola with tartness from the pomegranate syrup and golden raisins.

6-8 servings

3 cups rolled oats
1 cup unsalted pistachios, chopped
1 cup slivered almonds
¼ cup sesame seeds
2 tablespoons brown sugar
¼ cup honey
¼ cup pomegranate syrup
¼ cup vegetable or canola oil
1 teaspoon salt
1 cup golden raisins

- Preheat oven to 250°F.
- In a large bowl, mix together oats, pistachios, almonds, sesame seeds and brown sugar.
- In another bowl, mix together honey, pomegranate syrup, oil and salt. Pour over the oat and nut mixture and stir to combine.
- Pour mixture onto a cookie sheet that's lightly greased or lined with parchment paper. Bake for 1 hour and 15 minutes. Stir halfway through to ensure even cooking.
- When done, remove the cookie sheet and pour granola into a container with a tight-fitting lid. Add the raisins and stir to combine. Store in the airtight container for up to one week.
- To serve, sprinkle granola on top of your favorite yogurt or cereal.

Cardamom-Orange Pancakes with Rose Syrup

This is a beautiful, exotic twist on regular pancakes using cardamom, oranges and roses. If a Persian princess had to eat pancakes, this is what I imagine they'd be like! Try these out for your next Mother's Day brunch.

8 servings

Syrup:
1 cup brown sugar
¾ cup water
¼ cup rosewater
1 tablespoon orange zest

Pancake batter:
1 ½ cups all-purpose flour
3 ½ teaspoons baking powder
1 tablespoon granulated sugar
1 teaspoon ground cardamom
½ teaspoon salt
Zest of ½ an orange
1 ¼ cups milk
1 egg
3 tablespoons unsalted butter, melted

Garnish:
Dried rose petals

- In a small saucepan, bring the sugar and water to a boil. Reduce heat and simmer for 10 minutes. Add rosewater and orange zest and simmer for another 10 minutes. Remove from heat.
- Using a large sieve, sift together the dry pancake ingredients into a large mixing bowl. Add the wet ingredients and orange zest. Stir until no lumps remain in the batter.
- Grease a pan or griddle with butter, oil or cooking spray over medium heat. Drop batter onto the hot surface by the spoonful

and cook until pancakes are firm and golden brown on both sides.
- Serve drizzled with syrup. Garnish with dried rose petals if desired.

Eggs Benedict with Persian-Spiced Turkey Sausage, Lavash and Caramelized Onions

You really can't go wrong with the rich deliciousness of traditional eggs benedict, but I think this recipe is even better. With the caramelized onions and sweetly spicy sausage, the level of flavor is out of this world.

4 servings

32 (approximately 4-inch square) pieces of lavash bread

Sausage:
1 pound ground turkey
1 teaspoon ground cinnamon
1 teaspoon salt
1 teaspoon pepper
½ teaspoon ground ginger
½ teaspoon garlic powder
½ teaspoon fennel seeds
½ teaspoon chili powder
1 tablespoon vegetable or canola oil

Sauce:
4 egg yolks
1 tablespoon freshly squeezed lemon or lime juice
1 stick unsalted butter, melted
Salt and pepper to taste
4 tablespoons caramelized onions (homemade or store-bought)

Poached Eggs:
2 quarts water
1 teaspoon vinegar
8 eggs

For the sausages:

- In a large bowl, knead together the ground turkey and spices with your hands. Divide the meat into 8 equal portions. Form each portion into a round, flat sausage patty.
- Heat the oil in a pan over medium-high heat and fry the patties on each side until they are fully cooked and browned on the outside, about 3-4 minutes per side. Place them on a paper towel-covered plate and set aside.

For the sauce:

- In a small saucepan, whisk together the egg yolks and lemon or lime juice until thick. Place the saucepan on the stove over low heat for about 10 seconds, whisking the yolks vigorously throughout, and then remove them from the heat. Keep whisking. Repeat this two more times, being careful not to let the yolks get too hot (or else they will scramble).
- Remove from heat and gradually whisk in the melted butter until the sauce is thickened. Whisk in salt, pepper and the caramelized onions. Cover the sauce and set it aside.

To poach the eggs:

- In a heavy saucepan or pot, combine water and vinegar. Bring to a simmer.
- One by one, break eggs into a small bowl, cup or ramekin and slide them gently into the simmering water. Try to space them evenly.
- Poach eggs for about 3-4 minutes each (yolks will be slightly soft). Remove eggs from the water with a slotted spoon and set aside.

To serve:

- Create 8 stacks of 4 lavash pieces, and place 2 stacks on each plate.
- Lay a sausage patty on top of each stack, followed by a poached egg. Spoon the sauce over each stack and serve immediately.

Eggplant and Tofu Scramble

Eggplant is sadly overlooked at breakfast, but it can be a wonderful addition to omelets (or, in this case, a vegetarian tofu scramble). In this recipe, the *kashk* helps to bind the ingredients together and mimic the creaminess of eggs that tofu lacks.

2-4 servings

2 tablespoons canola oil
1 medium yellow onion, diced
1 garlic clove, minced
¼ teaspoon ground turmeric
¼ teaspoon ground cinnamon
¼ teaspoon ground cumin
½ large eggplant, peeled and finely diced
1 pound firm or extra-firm tofu, patted dry and crumbled
3 tablespoons *kashk*
¼ cup chopped flat-leaf parsley, plus more for garnish
½ cup crumbled feta cheese
Salt and pepper to taste

- In a large pan over medium heat, sauté the onion, and garlic in oil until the onion turns translucent. Add the turmeric, cinnamon and cumin and stir well. Add the eggplant and continue to cook, stirring, until the eggplant is tender, about 10 minutes.
- Add tofu and *kashk* and stir to combine. Cover and cook over low heat for an additional 5-7 minutes.
- Add parsley, feta, salt and pepper and stir until feta begins to melt. Garnish with parsley and serve with warm bread.

Fig, Honey and Goat Cheese Toasts

As a kid, toast with cream cheese and honey was one of my favorite snacks. Here is a slightly more sophisticated version of this delectable treat.

4 servings

8 (1-inch thick) baguette slices
Unsalted butter
Salt
8 ounces goat cheese, softened
8 Black Mission figs, sliced
Honey

- Preheat oven to 400°F.
- Butter each side of the bread slices and arrange them in a single layer on a baking sheet. Sprinkle with a tiny bit of salt and bake for 10 minutes.
- Remove the bread from the oven and let it cool to the touch. Spread each slice with goat cheese. Top with sliced figs, using a fork to press the figs down into the cheese, and a generous drizzle of honey.
- Serve with your morning tea or coffee.

Salads

~*~*~

Traditionally, certain raw vegetables were eaten alongside Persian dishes to enhance the flavors. Examples include fresh herbs, radishes, onions and scallions. Salads as we know them have become more popular over time.

Cucumber, Tomato and Onion Salad (Salad Shirazi)

Creamy Potato Salad with Chicken (Salad Olivieh)

Plum and Beet Salad with Sumac Vinaigrette

Artichoke Couscous Salad with Dill Yogurt Dressing

Lentil Salad

Garden Pasta Salad with Kale and Barberries

Chickpea and Peach Salad with Curried Balsamic Vinaigrette

Persian Fresh Fruit Salad

Pomegranate Marinated Flank Steak and Herb Salad

Quinoa Salad with Chickpeas, Herbs and Dates

Cucumber, Tomato and Onion Salad (*Salad Shirazi*)

Named for the city of Shiraz, this is the most popular salad in Persian cuisine. It is always satisfying, refreshing and delicious, demonstrating that sometimes, the simplest recipes are the best!

Shiraz is Iran's fifth-largest city and is known for its beautiful gardens and its poetry and literature (poets Hafez and Saadi were both from there). It is popular with tourists and is located within driving distance to the ruins of Persepolis, the tomb of Cyrus the Great, and other attractions.

2-4 servings

Dressing:
¼ cup olive oil
¼ cup freshly squeezed lemon juice
1 tablespoon finely chopped mint leaves (or 1 teaspoon dried mint leaves)
Salt and pepper to taste

Salad:
1 medium red onion, diced
2 large tomatoes, diced
1 large cucumber, peeled and diced

- Whisk together the dressing ingredients in a salad bowl. Add the onion, tomato and cucumber and stir to combine well.
- For best results, cover and refrigerate for at least 1-2 hours before serving. You can also make this a day ahead and refrigerate it until you're ready to serve.

Creamy Potato Salad with Chicken (*Salad Olivier*)

Salad olivier was originally created in Russia, but variations of the salad have become popular and have evolved in different countries as Russian émigrés have settled around the world. It is usually made with potatoes, vegetables, eggs, ham or chicken and mayonnaise.

This version, which is popular with Iranians, is made with potatoes, chicken, green peas, pickles, hard-boiled eggs and mayonnaise. The tartness of the pickles cuts through the richness of the potatoes, eggs and mayo and is absolutely irresistible. This is one of my favorite picnic foods.

6-8 servings

Dressing:
2 cups mayonnaise (you can substitute plain Greek–style yogurt)
¼ cup freshly squeezed lemon juice
2 tablespoons olive oil
1 teaspoon Dijon mustard
½ teaspoon paprika
Salt and pepper to taste

Salad:
4 large russet potatoes, boiled and peeled
4 eggs, hard boiled and finely diced
2 cups shredded cooked chicken
2 cups cooked green peas
2 large dill pickles, finely diced (can also use the equivalent amount of Persian pickles or gherkins)
1 carrot, diced or julienned (optional)

- In a large bowl, mash the potatoes well. Add the rest of the ingredients In a separate bowl, whisk together the dressing ingredients. Pour over the salad and stir well to combine everything. Taste and adjust seasoning as needed.
- For best results, cover and refrigerate for at least 2 hours before serving. This can be made and refrigerated one day ahead of serving.

Plum and Beet Salad with Sumac Vinaigrette

Crisp, juicy plums meet sweet beets and salty feta in this mouthwatering salad. The tangy sumac dressing draws out all of these flavors. Try bringing this to your next potluck or picnic and watch it disappear!

4-6 servings

4 ripe plums, diced, pits removed
2 (14-ounce) cans sliced red beets, diced
1 bell pepper, diced, seeds removed
1 small red onion, peeled and diced
¼ cup chopped basil leaves
¼ cup chopped tarragon leaves
½ cup crumbled feta cheese
¼ cup chopped walnuts

Dressing:
¼ cup olive oil
¼ cup balsamic vinegar
1 tablespoon honey
1 teaspoon ground sumac
1 teaspoon Dijon mustard
Salt and pepper to taste

- In a large bowl, place all of the salad ingredients.
- In a smaller bowl, whisk together the dressing ingredients and pour over the salad. Stir well to combine. For best results, chill the salad in the refrigerator for 2 hours before serving.

Artichoke Couscous Salad with Dill Yogurt Dressing

I love the smooth, delicate texture of artichoke hearts and their unique flavor. Neither artichokes nor couscous are traditional Persian ingredients; however, this light and delicious salad has a distinctly Persian twist with yogurt, dill, nuts and raisins.

4 servings

1 cup couscous
2 cups water
1 teaspoon salt
2 cups artichoke hearts (canned or frozen; if using frozen, cook first according to the package directions)
1 medium cucumber, peeled and diced
½ cup crumbled feta cheese
½ red onion, diced
¼ cup raisins
¼ cup slivered almonds
¼ cup chopped pistachios

Dressing:
⅓ cup plain yogurt
2 tablespoons olive oil
2 tablespoons freshly squeezed lemon juice
¼ cup chopped fresh dill or 1 tablespoon dried dill
2 garlic cloves, finely minced and smashed into a paste
Salt and pepper to taste

- Place couscous in a large bowl. In a saucepan, bring water to a boil and add salt. Pour the boiling water over the couscous, cover and wait for 5 minutes until the couscous has absorbed the water and expanded. Fluff it with a fork, then cover and refrigerate until no longer hot. Roughly chop the artichoke hearts and add them, along with the rest of the ingredients, to the couscous. In a separate bowl, whisk together the dressing ingredients and pour over the salad, stir well and serve.

Lentil Salad

This tasty, protein-rich salad is an easy and satisfying dish to make on a Sunday and eat throughout the week. The key thing to remember when making lentils for a salad is not to overcook them as you don't want the salad to become mushy.

4 servings

2 cups dried brown lentils
1 red onion, diced
1 scallion, chopped
1 carrot, diced
1 bell pepper, diced
1 celery stalk, diced
½ cup chopped flat-leaf parsley
¼ cup raisins
¼ cup capers

Dressing:
¼ cup olive oil
¼ cup freshly squeezed lemon juice
1 tablespoon Dijon mustard
1 teaspoon dried oregano
½ teaspoon dried thyme
¼ teaspoon garlic powder
¼ teaspoon ground turmeric
¼ teaspoon ground cumin
¼ teaspoon ground cinnamon
Salt and pepper to taste

- Rinse and drain lentils. Place them in a pot and cover with 2-3 inches of water. Cover and bring to a boil, then reduce heat and simmer for 15-20 minutes until lentils are mostly cooked but retain a slight bite. Drain and rinse them in cold water to stop the cooking process. Place the lentils in a large bowl and add the other salad ingredients. In a separate bowl, whisk together the dressing ingredients. Pour them over the salad and mix well. Refrigerate for at least 1 hour before serving.

Garden Pasta Salad with Kale and Barberries

I'm sure I'm not alone in saying that I could eat pasta every day and be perfectly happy. And, since pasta salads are so simple to make, that dream could easily become a reality! I'm always looking for inventive ways to use tart, tasty dried barberries, which are available in Persian markets. When added to salads they provide a nice bit of tartness similar to dried cranberries.

6-8 servings

1 (16-ounce) box rotini, fusilli or farfalle pasta, cooked and drained
2 cups chopped kale leaves
1 cup broccoli florets
1 small red onion, thinly sliced
½ cup diced carrots
¼ cup dried barberries, soaked in water for at least 15 minutes, drained and patted dry
2 tablespoons toasted sesame seeds

Dressing:
¾ cup mayonnaise
2 tablespoons olive oil
1 tablespoon Dijon mustard
Zest and juice of 1 lemon
Salt and pepper to taste

- In a large bowl, combine all of the salad ingredients.
- In a separate bowl, whisk together the dressing ingredients. Pour the dressing over the salad and stir well until everything is coated. Cover and refrigerate for at least 2 hours before serving. This salad can be made a day ahead and refrigerated until ready to serve.

Chickpea and Peach Salad with Curried Balsamic Vinaigrette

Curry spices add warmth to this sweet salad. Peaches are my favorite fruit, and I find them irresistible in this quick and delicious dish. Use fresh, ripe peaches for the most flavorful results.

4 servings

2 (15-ounce) cans chickpeas, drained and rinsed
2 ripe peaches, pits removed, diced
1 bell pepper, diced
½ small red onion, diced
½ cup chopped cilantro

Dressing:
¼ cup olive oil
¼ cup balsamic vinegar
1 teaspoon curry powder
Salt and pepper to taste

- In a large bowl, combine the salad ingredients.
- Whisk together the dressing ingredients in a separate bowl and pour the dressing over the salad. Stir well to combine, and serve.

Persian Fresh Fruit Salad

Fruit salad reminds me of warm summer afternoons. The addition of tart cherry juice adds a refreshing burst of flavor to this recipe.

4-6 servings

1 navel orange
1 apple, peeled, cored and sliced
1 cup red grapes
1 cup halved strawberries
1 cup cubed watermelon
1 cup cubed cantaloupe
¼ cup tart cherry juice

- Slice the top and the bottom off of the orange and stand it up on a cutting board. With a very sharp knife, slice off the peel and the bitter, white pith, following the curve of the fruit. Hold the orange over a large bowl and cut each orange segment out from between the membranes. Let the segments fall into the bowl.
- Add the rest of the ingredients and stir well. Cover and refrigerate for at least 2 hours before serving.

Pomegranate Marinated Flank Steak and Herb Salad

Strips of tender beef marinated in pomegranate syrup are served atop fresh herbs in this succulent dish.

6 servings

1 (1 ½ pound) flank steak
½ medium yellow onion, grated
⅓ cup pomegranate syrup
Salt and pepper to taste
Canola oil
2 cups arugula or spring mix
½ small red onion, sliced
½ medium cucumber, peeled and sliced
½ cup basil leaves
½ cup mint leaves
½ cup tarragon leaves
¼ cup chopped pistachios

Dressing:
¼ cup extra-virgin olive oil
¼ cup balsamic vinegar
1 tablespoon honey
1 tablespoon pomegranate syrup
1 teaspoon Dijon mustard
1 garlic clove, finely minced and smashed into a paste
Salt and pepper to taste

- In a shallow dish, combine the flank steak with the grated onion, pomegranate syrup, salt and pepper and rub the mixture all over the steak. Cover and refrigerate for 8 hours or overnight.
- Prepare your grill over medium-high heat. Brush grill rack with canola oil and lay the steak on top. Grill steak to desired level of doneness, then remove it from the grill and let it sit on a flat work surface for 10 minutes.

- In the meantime, combine the rest of the salad ingredients in a large bowl. In a separate bowl, whisk together the dressing ingredients. Pour all but 2 tablespoons of the dressing over the greens in the bowl and mix well.
- Slice the steak thinly on a slight diagonal, going against the grain.
- To serve, place salad on a platter and arrange steak slices on top. Drizzle a little bit of the reserved salad dressing over the steak. Serve immediately.

Quinoa Salad with Chickpeas, Herbs and Dates

This dish can be served warm or cold. It has a great balance of fresh flavors from the lemon, sumac and herbs combined with the rich sweetness of dates and the nuttiness of the quinoa and chickpeas.

4 servings

1 ½ cups water
1 ½ cups chicken stock (preferably homemade)
1 ½ cups quinoa
¼ cup olive oil
¼ cup freshly squeezed lemon juice
½ shallot, grated
1 teaspoon ground sumac
Salt and pepper to taste
1 (15-ounce) can chickpeas (garbanzo beans), drained and rinsed
½ cup pitted dates, chopped
¼ cup chopped basil leaves
¼ cup chopped parsley

- In a medium saucepan, add water, chicken stock and quinoa and bring to a boil. Lower heat to a simmer and let the quinoa continue cooking until all of the liquid has been absorbed. When the quinoa is done, transfer it to a large mixing bowl and refrigerate it until cold.
- Make the dressing by whisking together the olive oil, lemon juice, shallot, sumac, salt and pepper.
- Pour dressing, chickpeas, dates and herbs over the quinoa, stir well to combine, and serve.

Soups

~*~*~

A steaming bowl of hot soup can be your best friend on a chilly day. Similarly, a cold soup can quickly refresh you in the heat. This section includes recipes for both.

Noodle Soup with Beans and Herbs (Aash Reshteh)

Lamb and Barley Soup (Soup-e Jo)

Lentil Soup (Adaasi)

Chilled Yogurt Soup (Abdoogh Khiar)

Lamb, Potato and Bean Soup (Abgoosht)

Onion, Egg and Fenugreek Soup (Eshkeneh)

Yogurt, Mushroom and Split Pea Soup with Orzo (Aash-e Maast)

Roasted Carrot and Turnip Soup

My Mom's Chicken Noodle Soup

Artichoke and Herb Soup

Creamy Saffron Potato Soup

Noodle Soup with Beans and Herbs (Aash Reshteh)

A classic Persian dish, *aash reshteh* is a thick, hearty soup that tastes even better the next day, after all of the flavors have had a chance to blend.

6-8 servings

3 tablespoons canola oil
1 medium yellow onion, thinly sliced
6 large garlic cloves, minced
2 tablespoons dried mint leaves
½ teaspoon ground turmeric
1 cup dried green or brown lentils
Water
1 (15-ounce) can red kidney beans, drained and rinsed
1 (15-ounce) can chickpeas (garbanzo beans), drained and rinsed
2 cups flat-leaf parsley, chopped
2 cups cilantro, chopped
1 (10-ounce) package frozen chopped spinach, thawed
6 scallions, chopped
Salt and pepper to taste
2 tablespoons saffron water
6 ounces dried *reshteh* noodles (found in Persian grocery stores and online; you can substitute spaghetti or linguini broken up into 3-inch pieces)
Kashk (for garnish)

- In a pan, sauté the onions in oil over medium-high heat, stirring every 5 minutes or so, until they caramelize and turn a deep golden brown. Add the garlic, mint and turmeric, stir, and cook for another 4-5 minutes. Remove from heat and set aside.
- Place lentils and 8 cups of water in a large pot. Bring to a boil, then cover and cook over medium heat for 30 minutes or until lentils are just tender.

- Add the beans, herbs, spinach and scallions to the lentils. Cover and cook for another 30 minutes.
- Take about ⅓ cup of the fried onion mixture and add it to the soup. Season with salt and pepper to taste, add the saffron water and noodles, cover, and cook over medium-low heat for another 30 minutes. The soup is meant to be thick, but if it becomes too thick to stir, you can dilute it by adding boiling water.
- To serve, ladle the soup into a bowl. Top with some of the onion mixture and drizzle with 1-2 tablespoons of *kashk*. Serve with warm bread.

Lamb and Barley Soup (*Soup-e Jo*)

This soup tastes so rich and delicious thanks to the lamb broth, which really enriches the barley with a mouthwatering, savory flavor.

6-8 servings

1 bone-in lamb shank
1 medium yellow onion, diced
2 carrots, diced
1 celery stalk, diced
4 garlic cloves, finely minced and smashed into a paste
2 bay leaves
1 teaspoon freshly squeezed lime juice
¼ teaspoon ground turmeric
Salt and pepper to taste
Water
1 ½ cups pearled barley, soaked in water for 1 hour

- In a large pot, place everything except for the barley, and pour in enough water to cover it all by 3 inches. Bring to a boil, then reduce the heat to medium-low, cover, and cook for about 1 hour until the lamb is tender and falling off the bone. Remove the lamb from the pot and discard the bone. Shred the meat with your fingers and return it to the pot.
- Meanwhile, place the barley and 3 cups of water in another pot. Bring to a boil, then reduce heat to medium-low. Cover and cook for 45 minutes until barley is tender.
- Add the cooked barley (including its cooking liquid) to the pot with the lamb and simmer the soup over medium-low heat for 30 minutes. Serve the soup hot with warm bread on the side.

Lentil Soup (*Adaasi*)

Lentil soup is always a reliable go-to meal. It's easy, nutritious, and keeps well in the fridge for a few days. Earthy, rich lentils serve as a great base for adding layers of flavor with spices.

6-8 servings

1 tablespoon canola oil
1 yellow onion, diced
4 garlic cloves, minced
1 teaspoon ground turmeric
½ teaspoon ground cumin
¼ teaspoon ground cinnamon
2 cups green lentils
2 carrots, diced
2 celery stalks, diced
1 tablespoon tomato paste
2 teaspoons dried oregano
6 cups water (can substitute chicken or vegetable broth if desired)
Salt and pepper to taste
Golpar powder to taste

- In a large pot, heat the oil over medium-high heat. Sauté the onion, stirring every 5 minutes, until it turns golden brown. Add garlic and sauté for another 2-3 minutes. Add the turmeric, cumin and cinnamon and stir well.

- Add the lentils, carrots, celery, tomato paste, oregano and 6 cups of water. Bring to a boil, then cover, reduce heat to medium-low, and cook for 45 minutes.

- Check to make sure lentils are tender. Add salt, pepper and *golpar* to taste and stir well. Adjust seasoning if needed.

- Serve the soup hot with warm crusty bread or with rice, yogurt and herbs.

Chilled Yogurt Soup (*Abdoogh Khiar*)

This is a super light and refreshing soup. You won't mind eating bowl after bowl of this on a hot summer day!

4 servings

2 cups yogurt
2 medium cucumbers, peeled and grated
½ cup chopped walnuts
½ cup raisins
2 scallions, chopped
¼ cup basil leaves, chopped
¼ cup fresh tarragon leaves, chopped
¼ cup fresh mint leaves, chopped
Salt and pepper to taste
Cold water
Ice (optional)
Dried crushed rose petals, for garnish (optional)
Dried or day-old bread (optional)

- In a large bowl, add the yogurt and 1 cup of water and mix until very smooth.
- Add the cucumbers, walnuts, raisins, scallions and herbs. Add salt and pepper to taste. Stir well to combine.
- Add cold water, stirring continuously, until the soup reaches your desired consistency. Taste and adjust seasoning if needed. Cover and refrigerate for at least 2 hours before serving (alternatively, add ice cubes to make the soup cold).
- To serve, ladle the soup into bowls and sprinkle a pinch of dried rose petals on top. Serve with pieces of dried or day-old bread for crumbling into the soup.

Lamb, Potato and Bean Soup (*Abgoosht*)

Abgoosht (also called *dizi* after the earthenware pots in which it's traditionally cooked) is a hearty dish made of meat, potatoes and beans that consists of two distinct products: a broth and a mash. These can be eaten together or separately.

4-6 servings

Water
2 lamb shanks
1 (15-ounce) can navy or cannellini beans, drained and rinsed
1 (15-ounce) can chickpeas (garbanzo beans), drained and rinsed
2 yellow onions, quartered
4 garlic cloves, minced
2 large tomatoes, quartered
4 medium potatoes, peeled and quartered
1 teaspoon ground turmeric
½ teaspoon ground cinnamon
3 dried limes (*limoo amani*), soaked in hot water, pierced with a fork
1 heaping tablespoon tomato paste
Salt and pepper to taste

- In a large pot, bring 8 cups of water to a boil. Add all of the ingredients except for the salt and pepper. Reduce the heat to medium, cover, and cook for 2 hours or until the lamb is very tender and falling off the bone. Season with salt and pepper.

- Pour the broth through a strainer, into a large bowl, and set aside. Place the solids in a separate bowl. Remove the lamb bones and shred the meat with your fingers. With a potato masher, mash together the solids until they resemble a smooth mash.

- Ladle the broth into bowls and serve with the mash on the side, along with bread, yogurt, herbs and pickles. It's popular to crumble dried bread into the broth. The mash also makes a great sandwich filling (and the sandwiches can be dipped into the broth).

Onion, Egg and Fenugreek Soup (*Eshkeneh*)

Fenugreek is known and used throughout Persian and Indian cuisines for its medicinal value and unique flavor. For this soup, try finding fresh fenugreek if you can—its aromatic leaves will make a difference in the taste. Traditionally, water would be used instead of chicken stock, but I like the added flavor that the chicken stock provides.

6-8 servings

4 tablespoons canola oil or clarified butter (ghee)
2 yellow onions, sliced thinly
2 garlic cloves, minced
½ teaspoon ground turmeric
2 tablespoons all-purpose flour
1 cup chopped fresh fenugreek leaves, or ⅓ cup dried
4 cups low-sodium chicken stock
Salt and pepper to taste
3 eggs

- In a large pot, heat oil or ghee over medium-high heat. Add onions and sauté, stirring every 5 minutes or so, until they are caramelized and deep golden brown.
- Add garlic, turmeric, flour and fenugreek and cook, stirring, for another 2-3 minutes.
- Add the chicken stock and salt and pepper to taste. Bring to a boil, then reduce heat, cover, and simmer for 20 minutes.
- Crack the eggs into a bowl and whisk them together. Add 1 tablespoon of the soup broth to the eggs, whisking constantly, to temper them (slowly raise their temperature) and prevent them from scrambling when you add them to the soup. When the broth has been incorporated, add another tablespoon or two, whisking constantly.
- Pour the eggs into the soup a little bit at a time, constantly stirring the soup so that the eggs form long, thin strands while

cooking. The eggs should cook within the soup very quickly. The soup is done when all the eggs are incorporated.
- Taste and adjust seasoning if necessary. Serve with warm bread.

Yogurt, Mushroom and Split Pea Soup with Orzo

This recipe is my variation on *aash-e maast,* a traditional northern Iranian yogurt soup. For a more authentic version, replace the mushrooms with cooked chickpeas or lentils and the orzo with cooked rice.

6-8 servings

2 tablespoons canola oil or clarified butter (ghee)
1 yellow onion, grated, juices squeezed out
3 garlic cloves, minced
½ pound white mushrooms, chopped
1 tablespoon all-purpose flour
½ teaspoon ground turmeric
½ teaspoon ground cumin
4 cups low-sodium chicken or vegetable stock
4 cups yogurt, brought to room temperature
1 cup yellow split peas, picked over, rinsed and boiled until tender
2 scallions, chopped
1 cup cooked orzo pasta
½ cup chopped dill
½ cup chopped fresh cilantro
Salt and pepper to taste

- In a heavy-bottomed pot over medium-high heat, cook the onion, garlic and mushrooms in oil or ghee until the onion softens. Add the flour, turmeric and cumin and cook, stirring, for another 3-4 minutes. Add stock and bring to a boil, then reduce heat to medium-low.
- Temper the yogurt (gradually raise its temperature so it won't curdle when you add it to the soup): Place the yogurt in a large mixing bowl. Add a total of 1 cup of the hot stock to the yogurt by adding one tablespoon of stock at a time and stirring well before adding another. Do this until the stock becomes incorporated with the yogurt and the mixture is smooth and creamy. The yogurt should not curdle.

- Now, add the yogurt to the pot about ½ a cup at a time, stirring the soup constantly until it has all been incorporated and the soup is smooth.
- Add the rest of the ingredients to the soup and cook until the split peas and orzo are warmed through.
- Serve with warm, crusty bread and fresh herbs.

Roasted Butternut Squash Soup

Sweet butternut squash gets a fragrant lift from ginger and cardamom in this creamy, warming and nourishing autumn soup.

6-8 servings

2 medium butternut squash, halved lengthwise and seeds removed
2 tablespoons canola oil, divided
1 large yellow onion, chopped
4 garlic cloves, minced
1 teaspoon ground ginger
1 teaspoon ground cardamom
½ teaspoon ground cinnamon
½ teaspoon ground cumin
½ teaspoon ground turmeric
4 cups low-sodium chicken or vegetable stock
1 cup water
Salt and pepper to taste
1 tablespoon saffron water
⅓ cup heavy cream, brought to room temperature

Garnish (optional):
Dried rose petals
Pumpkin seeds
Sour cream

- Preheat oven to 425°F.
- Rub the squash halves with a tablespoon of oil and place them on a baking sheet. Bake until the squash is tender, about 1 hour. Remove from the oven and set aside.
- In the meantime, heat a tablespoon of oil in a large pot or Dutch oven over medium-high heat. Add the onion and garlic and sauté until onion turns translucent. Add the spices and cook, stirring, for another 2-3 minutes until fragrant.
- With a large spoon, scoop the butternut squash flesh out of its skin and add it to the pot. Then add the stock, water, salt and pepper. Cover and bring to a boil, then reduce heat and simmer for 10 minutes.
- Remove the pot from the heat and stir in the saffron water and heavy cream.

- Use an immersion blender to puree the soup until smooth. Alternatively, you can use a regular blender and work in batches.
- Serve with warm, crusty bread. Garnish each bowl, if desired, with a sprinkle of dried rose petals, some pumpkin seeds and a dollop of sour cream.

My Mom's Chicken Noodle Soup

Whether you're feeling under the weather or just need a warm, comforting meal, there's nothing that does the trick quite like chicken soup. It seems like everyone has a family recipe for this classic dish. This is the version my mom has always made, and it remains my favorite.

6-8 servings

1 tablespoon canola oil
1-1 ½ pounds bone-in chicken pieces
1 yellow onion, diced
2 carrots, diced
1 celery stalk, diced
4 garlic cloves, minced, smashed into paste
Salt and pepper to taste
½ teaspoon ground turmeric
Water
1 teaspoon tomato paste
8 ounces of your favorite short pasta (I like to use linguini broken up into 2-inch pieces)

- In a large pot, heat the oil over medium-high heat. Add the chicken, onion, carrots, celery and garlic and cook for 3-5 minutes until the onions soften. Add salt, pepper and turmeric and stir, cooking, for another minute.
- Add 8 cups of water to the pot and bring it to a boil, then reduce heat to a simmer. Cover the pot and let the soup cook for an hour and a half.
- In the meantime, cook and drain the pasta. Reserve 1 tablespoon of the hot pasta cooking water and mix it with the tomato paste until smooth.
- When the soup is done, add the tomato paste and stir well until it is incorporated throughout the soup. Add the cooked pasta to the soup and stir. Taste and adjust the seasonings as necessary, and serve.

Artichoke and Herb Soup

This delicious soup brings out the vibrant flavor of artichokes with the addition of fresh herbs, lemon and saffron.

4-6 servings

2 tablespoons olive oil
2 tablespoons unsalted butter
2 shallots, diced
1 celery stalk, diced
2-3 garlic cloves, minced
1 (9-ounce) package frozen artichoke hearts, thawed
4 cups low-sodium chicken or vegetable stock
1 cup chopped mint leaves
1 cup chopped cilantro
1 cup chopped parsley
2 scallions, chopped
Juice of 1 lemon
1 tablespoon saffron water
1 teaspoon ground sumac
Salt and pepper, to taste
Yogurt (optional)

- In a large pot over medium heat, melt the butter together with the olive oil. Add the shallots, celery, and garlic. Sauté until the shallots turn translucent.
- Add the thawed artichoke hearts and the stock and bring to a boil. Reduce heat and simmer for 20 minutes. Add the rest of the ingredients and simmer for another 5 minutes. Taste and adjust seasoning as needed.
- Puree the soup in a blender until smooth. Ladle into individual bowls and serve with a dollop of yogurt and some warm bread.

Creamy Saffron Potato Soup

Potato soup is such a rustic, comforting dish; it's one of those meals that make you feel like everything's going to be okay. Saffron adds another level of flavor to this smooth, indulgent soup.

6-8 servings

½ a stick of unsalted butter
1 yellow onion, diced
2 carrots, diced
3 celery stalks, diced
2 garlic cloves, diced
4 large russet potatoes, peeled and diced
2 tablespoons all-purpose flour
6 cups low-sodium chicken or vegetable stock
1 cup milk
½ cup heavy cream
Salt and pepper to taste
2 tablespoons saffron water
Minced parsley (for garnish)

- In a large pot, melt the butter over medium heat. Add the onion, carrots, celery and garlic and sauté until the onion is translucent. Add the potatoes and flour and cook, stirring, for another 3-4 minutes.
- Add the stock to the vegetables and bring it to a boil, then reduce heat and simmer for 15 minutes. Add the milk and simmer for another 5 minutes.
- Puree half of the soup in a blender, and then pour the puree back into the pot. Add the cream, salt, pepper, and saffron water and stir well to combine. Ladle into individual bowls, garnish with parsley, and serve.

Egg Entrees (*Kuku*)

~*~*~

Eggs bear a lot of symbolism in ancient Persian culture. Beautifully painted and decorated eggs, much like Easter eggs, are set out each spring for Persian New Year. They symbolized fertility and human life for the Zoroastrians who originally celebrated these traditions in Iran.

If you're unfamiliar with kuku, you can think of it as a Persian version of the frittata. It is a delicious vegetarian side dish that also serve as an entrée for any meal. A slice of kuku also makes a tasty sandwich filling.

For those who don't or can't eat egg yolks, you can make these with egg whites only. In addition, most of these recipes use all-purpose flour, but you can omit the flour or replace it with gluten-free flour if necessary.

I've written all of these recipes for baking in the oven, but you can also fry kuku in a skillet or on a griddle. You can also pour the batter into muffin pans and bake individual-sized portions.

Herb Kuku (Kuku Sabzi)

Potato and Leek Kuku (Kuku Sib Zamini)

Zucchini Kuku (Kuku Kadoo)

Eggplant Kuku (Kuku Bademjan)

Date and Sweet Potato Kuku

Broccoli and Asparagus Kuku

Dried Apricot and Almond Kuku

Kale Kuku

Herb Kuku (*Kuku Sabzi*)

This verdant dish is often served for Persian New Year, as herbs symbolize greenery and the renewal of life. The walnuts and barberries are optional, but I like the crunch that the walnuts provide and the tartness of the barberries as a contrast to the herbs.

4-6 servings

6 eggs
1 cup scallions, finely chopped
1 cup flat-leaf parsley, finely chopped
1 cup dill, finely chopped
½ cup chives, finely chopped
½ cup cilantro, finely chopped
¼ cup dried barberries, rinsed and patted dry
¼ cup chopped walnuts
2 tablespoons all-purpose flour
½ teaspoon ground turmeric
⅛ teaspoon baking powder
Salt and pepper to taste
Unsalted butter

- Preheat oven to 350°F.
- Crack open the eggs into a large mixing bowl and whisk together well.
- Add all ingredients to the eggs except for the butter, and stir to combine.
- Butter the bottom and sides of an oven-safe skillet. Pour in the kuku mixture and cover the skillet with aluminum foil. Bake for 45 minutes, removing the foil halfway through.
- Remove *kuku* from the oven and turn it over onto a platter. Serve warm or cold.

Leek and Potato Kuku (*Kuku Sib Zamini*)

A traditional potato *kuku* contains onions instead of leeks, but since leek and potato is such a delicious combination, I decided to use leeks in this recipe instead.

4-6 servings

1 large russet potato, peeled and sliced
1 tablespoon canola oil
1 leek, washed and finely chopped
½ teaspoon ground turmeric
¼ cup chopped chives or 1 tablespoon dried chives
2 tablespoons all-purpose flour
1 tablespoon saffron water
⅛ teaspoon baking powder
Salt and pepper to taste
6 eggs
Unsalted butter

- Preheat oven to 350°F.
- Boil or steam the potato slices until tender. Place them in a large mixing bowl and mash them roughly with a fork.
- Heat oil in a large pan over medium-high heat and add the leek. Cook until the leek has softened, then stir in the flour and turmeric and cook, stirring, for another 2 minutes. Remove from heat and combine with the potato. Add chives, saffron water, salt and pepper and stir well to combine. Add the baking powder and stir.
- In a separate bowl, crack open the eggs and whisk them together well. Pour the eggs over the potato and leek mixture and stir to combine.
- Butter the bottom and sides of an oven-safe skillet. Pour in the *kuku* mixture and cover the skillet with aluminum foil. Bake for 45 minutes, removing the foil halfway through.

- Remove *kuku* from the oven and turn it over onto a platter. Serve warm or cold.

Zucchini Kuku (*Kuku Kadoo*)

When life hands you fresh green zucchini, turn them into this tasty dish!

4-6 servings

2 zucchini, grated, juices squeezed out
1 tablespoon canola oil or clarified butter (ghee)
1 medium onion, sliced thinly
2 tablespoons all-purpose flour
6 eggs
1 teaspoon dried oregano
¼ teaspoon ground turmeric
⅛ teaspoon baking powder
Salt and pepper to taste
Unsalted butter

- Preheat oven to 350°F.
- In a pan over medium-high heat, fry the onion in oil or ghee until golden brown. Add the flour and cook, stirring, for 2 minutes. Remove from heat and drain on a paper towel.
- Crack open the eggs into a large mixing bowl and whisk together well. Add the rest of the ingredients to the eggs, except for the butter, and stir well.
- Butter the bottom and sides of an oven-safe skillet. Pour in the *kuku* mixture and cover the skillet with aluminum foil. Bake for 45 minutes, removing the foil halfway through.
- Remove *kuku* from the oven and turn it over onto a platter. Serve warm or cold.

Eggplant Kuku (*Kuku Bademjan*)

This rich and delicious *kuku* is sure to please. If desired, place thin tomato slices on top of the *kuku* before baking it to add a decorative pop of color.

4-6 servings

2 medium eggplants
1 yellow onion, thinly sliced
1 tablespoon canola oil or clarified butter (ghee)
4 garlic cloves, minced
2 tablespoons all-purpose flour
½ teaspoon ground turmeric
½ cup chopped flat-leaf parsley
6 eggs
1 tablespoon dried mint leaves
1 tablespoon saffron water
⅛ teaspoon baking powder
Salt and pepper to taste
Unsalted butter
1 tomato, sliced into ¼-inch thick slices (optional)

- Preheat oven to 350°F.
- Prick the eggplants with a fork and place them on a baking sheet. Roast them for an hour until tender. Let them cool to the touch, then peel away their skins, finely chop the flesh and set it aside.
- In a pan over medium-high heat, sauté the onion and garlic in oil or ghee until the onion turns golden brown. Add the flour and turmeric and cook, stirring, for another 2 minutes. Add the eggplant and parsley and stir well. Remove from heat.
- In a large bowl, crack open the eggs and whisk them together well. Add the eggplant mixture to the eggs, along with the mint, saffron water, baking powder, salt and pepper.
- Butter the bottom and sides of an oven-safe skillet. Pour in the *kuku* mixture and cover the skillet with aluminum foil.

(Optional step: Before covering, arrange thin tomato slices across the top of the *kuku* mixture.) Bake for 45 minutes, removing the foil halfway through.

- Remove *kuku* from the oven and turn it over onto a platter. Serve warm or cold.

Date and Sweet Potato Kuku

Dates are thought to provide a lot of energy, so many Iranians put them in breakfast omelets for a morning energy boost. The addition of sweet potato makes this *kuku* almost like a dessert—a great choice if you have a sweet tooth in the mornings.

4-6 servings

1 medium sweet potato
2 tablespoons unsalted butter, plus more for greasing the pan
1 cup dates, pitted and chopped
2 tablespoons all-purpose flour
¼ teaspoon ground cinnamon
6 eggs
⅛ teaspoon baking powder
Salt and pepper to taste
Unsalted butter

- Preheat oven to 350°F.
- Boil or steam the sweet potato until tender. Allow it to cool to the touch, and then peel it. Place it in a bowl and mash it well with a fork.
- In a pan, lightly sauté the dates in butter over medium heat until they soften. Add the flour and cinnamon and cook, stirring, for another 2-3 minutes. Add the mashed sweet potato and stir well.
- Crack open the eggs into a large mixing bowl and whisk together well. Add the date and sweet potato mixture as well as salt and pepper to taste. Add the baking powder and stir.
- Butter the bottom and sides of an oven-safe skillet. Pour in the *kuku* mixture and cover the skillet with aluminum foil. Bake for 45 minutes, removing the foil halfway through.
- Remove *kuku* from the oven and turn it over onto a platter. Serve warm or cold.

Broccoli and Asparagus Kuku

Tip: Use fresh, bright green asparagus spears that are firm and have tightly closed tips.

4-6 servings

2 tablespoons unsalted butter
1 tablespoon olive oil
6 green asparagus spears, chopped into 1-inch pieces
1 cup finely chopped broccoli florets
½ teaspoon ground turmeric
2 tablespoons all-purpose flour
6 eggs
¼ teaspoon garlic powder
⅛ teaspoon baking powder
Salt and pepper to taste
Unsalted butter

- Preheat oven to 350°F.
- In a pan over medium heat, melt the butter together with the olive oil. Add the asparagus and broccoli and sauté until dark green and tender, about 5 minutes. Add the turmeric and flour and cook for another minute, stirring constantly.
- In a separate bowl, crack open the eggs and whisk them together well. Add the asparagus and broccoli, garlic powder, baking powder, salt and pepper and stir well.
- Butter the bottom and sides of an oven-safe skillet. Pour in the *kuku* mixture and cover the skillet with aluminum foil. Bake for 45 minutes, removing the foil halfway through.
- Remove *kuku* from the oven and turn it over onto a platter. Serve warm or cold.

Dried Apricot and Almond Kuku

This dish is as beautiful as it is delicious. It's a symphony of flavors: sweet, nutty, with fresh herbs and savory onions.

4-6 servings

½ cup chopped or slivered almonds
2 tablespoons unsalted butter
1 tablespoon olive oil
1 small yellow onion, diced
⅔ cup chopped dried apricots
2 teaspoons chopped mint leaves
2 teaspoons chopped parsley
2 teaspoons chopped cilantro
2 tablespoons all-purpose flour
6 eggs
⅛ teaspoon baking powder
Salt and pepper to taste
Unsalted butter

- Preheat oven to 350°F. In a dry pan over medium heat, toast the almonds until fragrant. Set aside.
- Melt the butter together with the olive oil over medium-high heat. Add the onion and sauté until golden brown. Add the apricots and almonds and sauté for another 2-3 minutes. Add the mint, parsley and cilantro and stir well.
- In a separate bowl, crack open the eggs and whisk them together well. Add the apricot mixture, baking powder, salt and pepper and stir well.
- Butter the bottom and sides of an oven-safe skillet. Pour in the *kuku* mixture and cover the skillet with aluminum foil. Bake for 45 minutes, removing the foil halfway through.
- Remove *kuku* from the oven and turn it over onto a platter. Serve warm or cold.

Kale Kuku

Kale is in the superfood spotlight these days, but even if that trend fades, it will still be a tasty and nutritious leafy green.

4-6 servings

2 tablespoons unsalted butter
1 tablespoon olive oil
1 shallot, minced
2 cups kale leaves, chopped
2 tablespoons chopped fresh fenugreek leaves (or 2 teaspoons dried)
½ teaspoon ground turmeric
2 tablespoons all-purpose flour
6 eggs
½ teaspoon garlic powder
⅛ teaspoon baking powder
Salt and pepper to taste
Unsalted butter

- Preheat oven to 350°F.
- In a pan over medium heat, melt the butter together with the olive oil. Add the shallot, kale and fenugreek and sauté until the kale is dark and wilted (about 8 minutes). Add the turmeric and flour and cook, stirring, for another 2 minutes.
- In a separate bowl, crack open the eggs and whisk them together well. Add the kale mixture, garlic powder, baking powder, salt and pepper and stir well.
- Butter the bottom and sides of an oven-safe skillet. Pour in the *kuku* mixture and cover the skillet with aluminum foil. Bake for 45 minutes, removing the foil halfway through.
- Remove *kuku* from the oven and turn it over onto a platter. Serve warm or cold.

Stew Entrees (*Khoresht*)

~*~*~

Khoresht refers to a variety of braised stews. Served atop rice, it is the most common Persian entrée. One of the great pleasures of eating khoresht is letting your rice soak up its delicious juices. It is a wonderfully simple, rustic dish that is especially comforting during colder months.

Once you've mastered the basic idea, you can experiment with your favorite ingredients and create your own khoresht recipes. Each of the following recipes can be made vegan or vegetarian by omitting the meat and/or substituting it with beans and legumes.

Beef, Eggplant and Tomato Stew (Khoresht-e Bademjan)

Beef, Potato and Split Pea Stew (Khoresht-e Gheymeh)

Herb and Kidney Bean Stew with Mushrooms (Ghormeh Sabzi ba Gharch)

Chicken and Celery Stew (Khoresht-e Karafs)

Chicken in Pomegranate-Walnut Sauce (Fesenjan)

Lamb, Apricot and Apple Stew

Beef and Kumquat Stew

Chicken, Fennel and Tomato Stew

Chicken Curry Pot Pie

Some Tips on Making *Khoresht*

Using a slow cooker to prepare *khoresht* can save you time in the kitchen and add a lot of rich flavor. Prep your ingredients the night before or in the morning: sauté or caramelize your onions, and brown your meats, before adding them to the slow cooker. Certain types of *khoresht*, like *ghormeh sabzi*, also require herbs or other ingredients to be sautéed—make sure you sauté those before adding them to the slow cooker too. Dried beans can be added directly to the slow cooker after they have been soaked in water for 8 hours. Cook the *khoresht* in the slow cooker on low for 6-8 hours.

Khoresht can be frozen for up to 3 months and reheated before serving.

Finally, while *khoresht* is traditionally served with rice, you can substitute your favorite grain instead. In fact, I love to use certain types of *khoresht*, like *ghormeh sabzi*, *gheymeh* and others that have a relatively smooth texture, as sauces for pasta. It's an amazing combination!

Beef, Eggplant and Tomato Stew (*Khoresht-e Bademjan*)

In my opinion, this rich, flavorful stew is one of the most delicious ways to eat eggplant. The combination of eggplant and tomato is classic and familiar, but here it is kicked up a notch with Persian spices. I used beef for this recipe, but this stew can also be made with chicken, lamb or even lentils.

6-8 servings

2 large eggplants, peeled and sliced lengthwise into 2-inch wide strips
½ cup plus 2 tablespoons canola oil
1 yellow onion, diced
3 garlic cloves, minced
1 pound beef stew meat, cut into 1-inch or smaller cubes
1 teaspoon ground turmeric
½ teaspoon ground cinnamon
Salt and pepper to taste
3 cups water
2 large tomatoes, diced, or 1 (15-ounce) can diced tomatoes
1 heaping tablespoon tomato paste
Juice of 1 lime, or 1 tablespoon verjuice
2 tablespoons unripe grapes (optional)

- Sprinkle the eggplant slices with salt and set them aside for 30 minutes for the salt to draw out any bitterness. Rinse off the salt and pat the slices dry with a paper towel.
- In a large pan over medium-high heat, fry the eggplant slices in ½ cup of oil, turning once, until nicely browned on both sides. When done, place slices on a paper towel to drain off any excess oil.
- In a large pot or Dutch oven, heat 2 tablespoons of oil over medium-high heat. Add onions and cook until golden brown. Add garlic, beef, turmeric, cinnamon, salt and pepper. Cook, stirring, until the meat has browned on all sides.

- Add water, tomatoes, tomato paste, lime juice or verjuice, and the unripe grapes (if using). Bring the stew a boil and then reduce the heat to low. Cover and cook for 30 minutes.
- Layer the eggplant slices on top of the stew, cover, and cook for another 30 minutes or until the beef is very tender. Avoid stirring the stew after adding the eggplant as you don't want the eggplant to become mushy or break apart within the stew.
- Serve with rice, yogurt, and your favorite salad or herbs.

Beef, Potato and Split Pea Stew (*Khoresht-e Gheymeh*)

Gheymeh has an intoxicating sweet and sour flavor due to the cinnamon and the lime. The crispy potatoes on top of this hearty beef stew make it so much fun to eat.

4-6 servings

2 tablespoons canola oil
1 yellow onion, chopped
1 pound beef stew meat, cut into 1-inch or smaller cubes
1 teaspoon ground turmeric
½ teaspoon ground cinnamon
Salt and pepper to taste
1 cup yellow split peas, picked over and rinsed
2 heaping tablespoons tomato paste
3 cups water
4 dried limes (*limoo amani*), soaked in hot water and pierced with a fork
Store-bought fried potato sticks (for garnish)

- In a large pot or Dutch oven, heat oil over medium-high heat and add the onion. Cook until the onion turns golden brown.
- Add beef, turmeric, cinnamon, salt and pepper and cook, stirring often, until the meat has browned on all sides.
- Add yellow split peas and tomato paste. Cook for another 5 minutes, stirring often.
- Add water and dried limes. Turn the heat to low, cover, and cook for 1 hour or until the meat is very tender.
- When serving, sprinkle a layer of fried potato sticks over the stew. Serve with rice.

Herb and Kidney Bean Stew with Mushrooms (*Ghormeh Sabzi ba Gharch*)

This recipe, featuring mushrooms, is a vegetarian departure from traditional *ghormeh sabzi* (which is usually made with beef). The meaty quality of mushrooms makes them a great substitute.

If you want to make it the traditional way, using meat instead of mushrooms, use about a pound of cubed beef stew meat. Brown the meat in the same way as the mushrooms, but let the stew simmer for half an hour longer.

If you're using dried kidney beans instead of canned, then soak them overnight and cook them separately, until they are tender, before adding them to the stew.

4-6 servings

3 tablespoons canola oil, divided
2 cups flat-leaf parsley, finely chopped
2 cups cilantro, finely chopped
2 cups chives, finely chopped
1 cup fresh fenugreek leaves, finely chopped (or 4 tablespoons dried fenugreek leaves)
4 scallions (green portions only), finely chopped
1 medium yellow onion, peeled and diced
1 pound white mushrooms, chopped
1 teaspoon ground turmeric
Salt and pepper to taste
2 dried limes (*limoo amani*), soaked in hot water and pierced with a fork (or the juice of 2 limes)
Water
1 (15-ounce) can red kidney beans, drained and rinsed

- In a large sauté pan, heat 1 tablespoon of oil over medium-high heat and add the herbs and scallions. Sauté until they soften and turn dark green, about 5 minutes. Turn off the heat.
- In a large pot or Dutch oven, sauté the onion in 2 tablespoons of oil over medium-high heat until golden brown.

- Add the mushrooms, turmeric, salt and pepper (to the onion). Stir well and continue to sauté until the mushrooms turn brown and soften, about 5 minutes.
- Add the sautéed herb and scallion mixture and the dried limes or lime juice to the pot (with the onion and mushrooms). Add enough water to just cover everything, and bring it to a boil. Reduce heat to low, add the kidney beans, and cook for 25-30 minutes. Serve over rice with a side of yogurt and *torshi*.

Chicken and Celery Stew (*Khoresht-e Karafs*)

Celery can do so much more than flavor soups, complement chicken wings and add crunch to salads. It is the star of this dish, a childhood favorite of mine, and you will be pleasantly surprised by the flavor that it will take on with the meat, herbs and limes. This dish can also be made with beef or lamb.

4-6 servings

3 tablespoons canola oil, divided
6 celery stalks, chopped into 1-inch pieces
2 cups flat-leaf parsley, chopped
1 cup mint leaves, chopped
1 ½ pounds chicken thighs or leg quarters
Salt and pepper to taste
1 yellow onion, chopped
2 garlic cloves, minced
1 teaspoon ground turmeric
¼ teaspoon ground cinnamon
Water
1 tablespoon saffron water
3 dried limes (*limoo amani*), soaked in hot water and pierced with a fork

- Heat 1 tablespoon of oil in a large pan over medium-high heat. Add the celery, parsley and mint. Sauté for 3-4 minutes or until the celery just begins to soften. Remove from heat and set aside.
- In a large pot or Dutch oven, heat 1 tablespoon of oil over medium-high heat. Season the chicken pieces with salt and pepper and place them in the hot oil. Cook, turning over once, until the chicken has browned on both sides. Place the chicken on a plate and set it aside.
- Add another tablespoon of oil to the pot and sauté the onion, stirring every few minutes, until golden brown and

caramelized. Add the garlic, turmeric and cinnamon, stir well, and cook for another 2-3 minutes.

- Place the chicken back into the pot with the onions and add two cups of water. Cover and bring to a boil, then reduce heat to medium-low and simmer for 15 minutes. After 15 minutes, add the celery mixture, saffron water, dried limes, and salt and pepper to taste. Cover and simmer for an extra 30 minutes.
- Serve with rice, yogurt and your favorite salad or herbs.

Chicken in Pomegranate-Walnut Sauce (*Fesenjan*)

Fesenjan is one of my very favorite dishes—it's the perfect combination of rich, sweet, sour and savory. This is also excellent with duck instead of chicken.

6-8 servings

4 cups chopped walnuts
Water
1 cup pomegranate syrup
1 tablespoon canola oil
1 yellow onion, diced
1 whole chicken, rinsed, giblets removed, cut into 8 pieces (alternatively, you can use chicken thighs or leg quarters)
1 teaspoon salt, plus more to taste
Black pepper to taste
2 tablespoons granulated sugar

- Working in batches, toast the walnuts in a large skillet over low heat by heating them gently through until they become fragrant. Then, place the walnuts in a food processor and grind them until they resemble fine crumbles.

- In a pot, combine the ground walnuts with 2 cups of water. Cook over low heat until a layer of oil forms over the walnuts. Add the pomegranate syrup and 1 teaspoon salt. Stir well, remove from heat, and set aside.

- In a separate pot or Dutch oven, sauté the onion in 1 tablespoon of oil over medium-high heat until caramelized and deep golden brown. Season the chicken with salt and pepper on both sides. Add the chicken pieces into the pot with the onion and cook over medium-high heat, turning once, for 5-7 minutes on each side.

- Pour the walnut-pomegranate sauce over the chicken and bring to a boil. Reduce the heat to medium-low, cover, and simmer for 1-1.5 hours. Add the sugar 10 minutes before the end and stir well. Serve over rice.

Lamb, Apricot and Apple Stew

Something about this meal just screams 'autumn' to me. I designed this recipe as an ode to my favorite season, rich with fragrant lamb, fruit and warming spices.

4-6 servings

2 tablespoons canola oil
1 yellow onion, chopped
4 garlic cloves, minced
½ teaspoon ground turmeric
½ teaspoon ground cinnamon
1 ½ pounds lamb stewing meat, cubed
Salt and pepper to taste
Water
3 Granny Smith apples, peeled, cored, and sliced
2 tablespoons brown sugar
Juice of 1 lemon
1 teaspoon apple cider vinegar
1 cup dried apricots, chopped
1 tablespoon saffron water

- In a large pot or Dutch oven, heat the oil over medium-high heat. Add the onion and sauté until caramelized and deep golden brown. Add the garlic, turmeric, and cinnamon and cook, stirring, for another 2-3 minutes until fragrant.
- Add the lamb to the onion and cook until it has browned on all sides. Season with salt and pepper, and then add 2 cups of water. Cover the pot and bring stew to a boil; then, reduce heat to medium-low and simmer for 30 minutes.
- In the meantime, combine the apple slices, brown sugar, lemon juice, vinegar and dried apricots in a separate bowl and mix well. After 30 minutes, add the fruit mixture and the saffron water to the lamb. Cover and simmer for another 30 minutes until apples and meat are tender. Serve over rice.

Beef and Kumquat Stew

I love kumquats. These bite-sized citrus fruits are sweet, sour and just a little spicy. Kumquats are wholly edible, including their peels. This recipe would also taste great with chicken and lamb.

4-6 servings

½ cup slivered almonds
2 tablespoons canola oil
1 yellow onion, diced
1 pound beef stewing meat, cut into 1-inch cubes
4 garlic cloves, minced
1 teaspoon ground turmeric
1 teaspoon ground cumin
½ teaspoon ground cinnamon
1 ½ cups fresh kumquats, halved lengthwise and seeds removed
1 tablespoon brown sugar
Zest and juice of 1 orange
Salt and pepper to taste
Water
½ cup chopped mint leaves (for garnish)

- In a dry pan over medium heat, toast the almonds until fragrant. Remove from heat and set aside.
- In a large pot or Dutch oven over medium-high heat, add the oil and the onion and sauté until the onion is caramelized. Add the beef, garlic, turmeric, cumin and cinnamon and cook, stirring, until the beef is browned on the outside.
- Add the rest of the ingredients, including the toasted almonds, and 2 cups of water. Bring it to a boil, then cover and reduce heat to medium-low. Simmer for 1 hour. Garnish with mint leaves. Serve with rice, yogurt, salad, *torshi* and fresh herbs.

Chicken, Fennel and Tomato Stew

The anise flavor of fennel is balanced out nicely by the ingredients in this delicate stew.

4-6 servings

2 tablespoons olive oil
2 tablespoon unsalted butter
1 yellow onion, thinly sliced
1 fennel bulb, thinly sliced
6 chicken leg quarters or thighs
Salt and pepper to taste
½ teaspoon ground turmeric
6 garlic cloves, minced
2 cups low-sodium chicken stock
1 cup cherry tomatoes, halved
1 teaspoon dried thyme

- In a large pot or Dutch oven over medium-high heat, melt the butter together with the oil. Season the chicken pieces with salt and pepper and place them in the oil and butter until they are browned. Add the onion and fennel and cook until softened, about 4-5 minutes.
- Add salt, pepper, turmeric and garlic cloves and cook for 2-3 more minutes. Add the stock, tomatoes and thyme and bring to a boil, then cover, reduce the heat to medium-low, and simmer for 40 minutes. Serve with rice, yogurt, salad, *torshi* and herbs.

Chicken Curry Pot Pie

Chicken curry *khoresht* makes a terrific savory filling for a unique and flavorful pot pie.

6-8 servings

2 tablespoons butter
1 yellow onion, diced
3 garlic cloves, minced
4 tablespoons curry powder
4 boneless, skinless chicken breasts, cubed
Salt and pepper to taste
1 ½ cups raw or roasted unsalted cashews, ground in a food processor or blender
Water
1 tablespoon saffron water
2 tablespoons freshly squeezed lemon juice
2 unbaked, store-bought 9-inch pie crusts with tops (or use frozen phyllo dough sheets instead of tops)

- Follow the directions on the package to thaw your pie crusts (if necessary) and preheat the oven to the required temperature.
- In a large pot or Dutch oven, sauté onion in butter over medium-high heat until the onion turns golden brown. Add curry powder and stir well.
- Add the chicken pieces and sauté until the chicken has completely cooked through, about 10-15 minutes. Season with salt and pepper.
- Add the ground cashews and 2 cups of water. Stir well, reduce the heat to low, and simmer for 30 minutes, stirring occasionally. Once the stew has thickened, add the saffron water and lime juice. Cook for another 10 minutes.
- Ladle the stew into the bottom pie crusts. Cover with top crusts or frozen phyllo dough, seal edges, and trim away any excess dough. To allow steam to escape, make several small slits in the top crusts with a knife.

- Bake in the preheated oven according to your crust's package directions, or until the crust is golden brown and the filling is bubbly. Let cool for 10-15 minutes before serving.

From the Grill: Kabobs & More

~*~*~

There's nothing like a juicy kabob straight off the grill. Believed to have originated in the Eastern Mediterranean before spreading geographically, kabobs are highly popular in Persian cuisine. They are equally ubiquitous at restaurants, street vendors and family cookouts.

Ground Lamb Kabobs (Koobideh)

Saffron-Lime Chicken Kabobs (Joojeh)

Beef Tenderloin Kabobs (Barg)

Pan-Fried Beef Kabobs (Maytabeh)

The Ultimate Kabob Burger

Savory Veggie Kabobs

Fresh Grilled Fruit Kabobs

Yogurt-Marinated Tofu Kabobs

Pomegranate-Citrus Grilled Shrimp Tacos

The Persian Kabob-urrito

Types of Kabobs

Kabob Barg

A *barg* kabob consists of thin strips of marinated beef tenderloin, lamb, or chicken breast, skewered closely together and grilled. Each piece of meat is about 2 inches wide and ½ inch thick. *Barg* is the Persian word for leaf, and these kabobs can be thought of as thinner "leaves" of meat grilled together on the skewer to form a long, flat kabob.

Kabob Koobideh

Koobideh means "pounded," and as you might guess, a *koobideh*-style kabob uses ground meat (usually beef or lamb). The meat is seasoned and pressed onto a kabob skewer before grilling.

Soltani

In Persian restaurants you will often see kabobs offered *soltani* style. This means that you get a skewer each of *barg* and *koobideh*. Like a sultan, you don't even have to choose between them!

Joojeh Kabob

Joojeh refers specifically to young chickens, whose meat is tenderer and was traditionally used for making this kabob. However, nowadays people use any time of chicken to make *joojeh* kabob, which is made by grilling pieces of chicken that have been marinated in a yogurt and saffron-based marinade.

Shishlik

Beef or lamb kabobs made of larger chunks of meat.

Serving Kabobs Persian-Style

A full kabob meal might include the following:

- Freshly grilled kabobs
- Ground sumac for sprinkling on kabobs
- Rice
- Lavash bread (Tip: Pile kabobs on top of lavash bread right after they're done grilling, and place some more lavash on top. The bread not only helps keep the kabobs warm, but it soaks up the juices from the meat and becomes a flavorful delight on its own.)
- Chargrilled whole tomatoes (I love to break up the tomato with my fork so that the rice or bread absorbs the tomato juices along with the meat juices and sumac—to me, this is the ultimate comfort food!)
- Salad (especially Cucumber, Tomato and Onion Salad: see recipe on page 70)
- Yogurt
- Pickles
- Fresh herbs

Tender Ground Meat Kabobs (*Koobideh*)

These are a crowd-pleasing hit at any cookout.

4-6 servings

2 pounds finely ground lamb or beef (I recommend grinding it twice or having your butcher do so. For best results, use ground meat that contains no less than 15%-20% fat.)
1 large yellow onion
1 teaspoon garlic powder
½ teaspoon ground turmeric
Salt and pepper to taste

Basting liquid:
4 tablespoons unsalted butter, melted
1 tablespoon saffron water

Prep:

- Peel and chop the onion and puree it in a blender. Squeeze the juice out of the onion puree using cheesecloth. Place the onion puree into a large mixing bowl.
- Add all ingredients to the onion puree and knead the mixture very well with your hands. The more you knead, the lighter the texture of the kabob will be. The mixture should not be too dry and should have a slight elasticity and stickiness, but it shouldn't be sticking to your hands. The key is to have the mixture sticky enough to adhere to the skewer blades during grilling and not fall off, but you don't want there to be any excess liquid. If the mixture is too dry, you can add some of the onion juice to it. If it's too wet, you can add more meat or some unseasoned bread crumbs.
- Cover and place the meat mixture in the refrigerator to marinate for at least 2 hours (preferably up to 1 day). The longer refrigeration will help hold the kabobs together on the grill and provide more flavor. Remove it from the fridge (and start your charcoal, if using a charcoal grill) 30 minutes prior to grilling.

Grilling:

- You will use a tennis-ball sized amount of meat for each kabob skewer. Using your hands, squeeze the meat flat around the blade of the skewer, leaving room at the top and bottom. With your fingers, squeeze the meat every inch or so along the length of the skewer to form slight ridges. If the meat sticks to your hands as you're doing this, moisten your hands with the reserved onion juice or some water.

- Make sure the grill is very hot before placing the skewers on the grill. Turn each skewer over every minute during grilling until the kabobs are browned on both sides and cooked through. Baste with a mixture of the melted butter and saffron water.

- Use a wide piece of lavash bread as a mitten to grip each kabob and slide it off of the skewer when it's done. Place the bread on top of the finished kabobs to keep them warm until you're done grilling them all. Serve hot with bread, rice, yogurt, pickles, herbs and salad.

Saffron-Lime Chicken Kabobs (*Joojeh*)

The marinade for these classic kabobs produces chicken that is moist, flavorful and delicious.

4-6 servings

Marinade:
1 large yellow onion
1 cup yogurt
4 tablespoons olive oil
4 tablespoons freshly squeezed lime juice
2 tablespoons saffron water
Salt and pepper to taste

Kabobs:
2 pounds boneless, skinless chicken breasts, cut into 2-inch pieces

Basting liquid:
2 tablespoons unsalted butter, melted
2 tablespoons freshly squeezed lime juice

- Peel and grate the onion into a large bowl. Combine the rest of the marinade ingredients with the onion. Add the chicken and mix well until chicken pieces are well-coated. Cover and refrigerate for 6-8 hours or overnight.
- Remove the chicken from the refrigerator and heat your grill until very hot. Skewer 6-8 pieces of chicken close together on each of your metal kabob blades, leaving room at the top and the bottom. Place them on the hot grill and cook, turning frequently, until the chicken is cooked through, about 20 minutes. Baste the kabobs with the butter and lime mixture. Serve hot with rice, bread, yogurt, salad, herbs and pickles.

Beef Tenderloin Kabobs (*Barg*)

Tenderloin produces wonderfully tender kabobs that nearly melt in your mouth with softness.

4-6 servings

Marinade:
1 large yellow onion
1 tablespoon saffron water
½ cup yogurt
2 tablespoons olive oil
2 garlic cloves, crushed
Salt and pepper to taste

Kabob:
2 pounds beef tenderloin fillet, sliced into small, thin strips approximately ½ inch thick and 1 ½ to 2 inches long

Basting liquid:
2 tablespoons unsalted butter, melted
2 tablespoons freshly squeezed lime juice

- Peel and grate the onion into a large bowl. Combine the rest of the marinade ingredients with the onion. Add beef and mix well to coat with marinade. Cover and place beef in the refrigerator to marinate for 6-8 hours or overnight.
- Preheat your grill until it's very hot. When you're ready to grill, slide the beef strips together onto the blade of a metal kabob skewer and push them as close together as possible. Make sure to leave room on either end of the skewer.
- Turn kabobs frequently during grilling and brush each side with the butter and lime juice until the beef is done (for medium-rare, grill for 3-4 minutes on each side).
- Use a piece of lavash bread to grab the meat and slide it off the skewer. Cover the kabob with the bread to keep it warm until all of the kabobs are done and ready to serve. Serve hot with rice, bread, yogurt, pickles, herbs and salad.

Pan-Fried Beef Kabobs (*Maytabeh*)

Kabob maytabeh (meaning 'pan kabob') is a classic easy home-cooked dish. These kabobs take less time and effort than the grilled variety, but they are just as delicious.

4 servings

1 ½ pounds ground beef
1 medium yellow onion
1 teaspoon ground turmeric
Salt and pepper to taste
1 teaspoon canola oil

- Peel and grate the onion into a large bowl. Squeeze out juices using cheesecloth. Add the meat, turmeric, salt and pepper. Knead the mixture well with your hands (remember, the more you knead, the lighter and airier the kabob's texture will be).
- Grease the bottom of a large skillet with oil. Place the meat mixture into the pan and, using your hands, flatten it out against the bottom of the skillet in an even layer.
- Cook the meat over medium-high heat for about 10 minutes. Once the bottom of the meat has set, use a knife or spatula to cut the meat patty into either strips (about 1-2 inches wide) or triangles (like a pizza). Then, flip each piece over and cook the other side for another 10 minutes or so until the meat is fully cooked through.
- Serve kabobs with sumac for sprinkling, along with rice, bread, yogurt, salad, herbs and pickles.

The Ultimate Kabob Burger

With tart sumac, smoky grilled tomatoes, fresh herbs and spicy onions, this mouthwatering hamburger contains all of the essential flavors of a Persian kabob feast. For best results, use meat that contains at least 15-20% fat. I recommend using twice-ground meat to give the burgers a finer texture, which will be more similar to a kabob.

4 servings

1 medium yellow onion, peeled and roughly chopped
1 ½ pounds ground beef or lamb
2 teaspoons dried mint leaves
2 teaspoons ground sumac plus ½ teaspoon
½ teaspoon ground turmeric
Salt and pepper to taste
2 Roma tomatoes, halved lengthwise
½ cup plain yogurt
2 teaspoons chopped dill leaves
4 large hamburger buns (preferably with sesame seeds)
1 red onion, peeled and thinly sliced
12 dill pickle slices
½ cup fresh basil leaves

- Puree the onion in a food processor. Dump the contents into cheesecloth and squeeze out the juices. Place the solids in a large mixing bowl.
- To the onion, add the meat, dried mint, 2 teaspoons of sumac, turmeric, salt and pepper. Use your hands to knead it all together well and form the mixture into 4 equal-sized patties.
- Preheat your grill until very hot. Place the patties on the grill and cook them to your desired level of doneness. Place the tomato halves on the grill, skin sides down, and cook until their skins blister and black marks appear.
- In a small bowl, mix together the yogurt, dill and remaining sumac with a pinch of salt. Toast the hamburger buns and spread the bottom and top of each bun with a spoonful of this yogurt sauce.
- On each bun, stack a burger patty, half of a grilled tomato, a few red onion slices, three pickle slices and some basil leaves. Serve immediately.

Savory Veggie Kabobs

When it comes to kabobs, meat doesn't have to have all the fun.

4 servings

Marinade:
¼ cup olive oil
¼ cup lemon juice
1 tablespoon saffron water
Salt and pepper to taste

Kabobs:
2 large red onions, quartered
2 green bell peppers, seeds removed and quartered
4 Roma tomatoes
2 zucchini, cut into 2-inch chunks
1 large eggplant, cut into 2-inch pieces
12 white mushrooms

- Combine marinade ingredients in a large bowl and add the vegetables. Mix well to evenly coat the vegetables in marinade. Cover and refrigerate for 1-2 hours.
- Preheat your grill until very hot. Skewer the vegetables onto metal kabob skewers, leaving space at the top and bottom. Grill, turning once, until the veggie skins blister and grill marks appear.
- Serve with your choice of meat, rice, bread, yogurt, salad, herbs and pickles.

Fruit Kabobs

The warm, sweet juiciness of fruit contrasted with the smoky flavor from the grill is utterly delectable. These can be served as a side dish or even as a dessert (try grilled fruit on ice cream!).

4 servings

Marinade:
¼ cup olive oil
¼ cup lime juice
1 tablespoon saffron water
½ teaspoon salt

Kabobs:
½ a pineapple, peeled and cut into 2-inch chunks
1 mango, peeled and cut into 2-inch chunks
2 peaches or nectarines, halved and pitted
2 plums, halved and pitted
12 strawberries, leaves removed
1 cup cubed watermelon
1 cup cubed cantaloupe

- Combine marinade ingredients in a large bowl. Add fruit and mix well until fruit is evenly coated with marinade. Cover and refrigerate for 1-2 hours.
- Preheat your gas or charcoal grill. Skewer fruit onto metal kabob skewers, leaving space at the top and bottom. When the grill is hot, grill the fruit kabobs, turning often, until grill marks form. Keep a close eye on them and make sure they don't burn (fruit burns easily due to its high sugar content). Serve immediately.

Spicy Tofu Kabobs

Make sure you use extra-firm tofu and pat it dry before grilling to prevent it from breaking apart on the grill.

4 servings

Marinade:
2 tablespoons olive oil
2 tablespoons lime juice
2 tablespoons yogurt
1 teaspoon onion powder
1 teaspoon garlic powder
1 teaspoon paprika
½ teaspoon cayenne pepper
Salt and pepper to taste
Canola oil

Kabob:
2 (14-ounce) packages extra-firm tofu, drained, patted dry, and cut into 2-inch cubes

- Combine marinade ingredients in a large bowl. Add tofu pieces and mix together until tofu is coated evenly with marinade. Cover and refrigerate for 30 minutes.
- Preheat your grill and brush the grill rack with oil. Gently skewer the tofu pieces closely together onto flat metal kabob skewers. Grill tofu, turning once, until grill marks form, about 5 minutes on each side.
- Serve with your choice of rice, bread, grilled vegetables, salad, yogurt, herbs and pickles.

Pomegranate-Citrus Grilled Shrimp Tacos

Seafood tacos are a personal favorite of mine. This recipe is a great way to try succulent shrimp tacos with a Persian twist.

4 servings

Marinade:
2 tablespoons olive oil
2 tablespoons lime juice
2 tablespoons pomegranate syrup
2 tablespoons orange juice
½ teaspoon garlic powder
½ teaspoon ground cumin
½ teaspoon ground turmeric
¼ teaspoon ground cinnamon
Salt and pepper to taste

2 pounds jumbo shrimp, peeled and deveined
2 tablespoons mayonnaise
Salt to taste
1 cup shredded cabbage
2 radishes, grated
2 scallions, chopped
¼ cup chopped cilantro
¼ cup chopped flat-leaf parsley
1 teaspoon nigella seeds
8 small flour or corn tortillas
1 cup Pomegranate Salsa (see recipe on page 201)

- In a large bowl, combine the marinade ingredients. Add the shrimp and mix well so that all of the shrimp is evenly coated in marinade. Cover and refrigerate for 1-2 hours.
- In the meantime, in a small bowl, combine the mayonnaise with a pinch of salt. Add the cabbage, radishes, scallions, cilantro, parsley and nigella seeds. Stir well to combine.

- Preheat a gas or charcoal grill. Gently skewer the shrimp onto metal kabob skewers. Grill, turning frequently, until the shrimp are no longer pink (about 5 minutes).
- To assemble the tacos, place a few shrimp and some of the cabbage mixture inside each tortilla and top each with a spoonful of Pomegranate Salsa. Serve immediately.

The Persian Kabob-urrito

Is there anything that can't be wrapped up in a tortilla and still taste scrumptious? The answer is probably no, and once you taste this burrito you'll be reaching for all kinds of other fillings to satisfy your exotic burrito cravings.

4 servings

4 large flour tortillas
1 cup Persian rice of your choice
4 skewers kabob of your choice
1 cup Cucumber, Tomato and Onion Salad (see recipe on page 70)
1 cup crumbled feta cheese
4 tablespoons plain yogurt
¼ cup mint leaves
Ground sumac

- Lay the tortillas on a flat surface and fill each with ¼ cup of rice, a skewer of kabob, ¼ cup each of the salad and the cheese, 1 tablespoon of yogurt, and a few mint leaves. Sprinkle each burrito with sumac. Starting from the sides, fold the tortilla inward and then roll it closed. Serve with tortilla chips and Pomegranate Salsa (see recipe on page 201) or Creamy Fried Eggplant Dip (see recipe on page 193).

Additional Entrees

~*~*~

Braised Lamb Shanks in Garlic Broth (Mahicheh)

Herb-Stuffed Roasted Fish (Mahi)

Jumbo Meat and Rice Meatballs (Koofteh Berenji)

Stuffed Bell Peppers (Dolmeh Felfel)

Smoked Eggplant and Tomato Casserole with Garlic and Eggs (Mirza Ghasemi)

Sausage and Potato Sandwiches (Sosis Bandari)

Persian-Style Spaghetti with Meat Sauce (Macaroni)

Fish with Spicy Tamarind Sauce

Beef Tongue Sandwiches

Iranian-Style Pizza

Persian-Inspired Nachos

The Persian Muffuletta

Braised Lamb Shanks in Garlic Broth (*Mahicheh*)

You won't be able to resist taking bite after bite of tender, velvety lamb that falls apart at the touch of your fork. Served with fragrant, buttery rice soaked in the cooking juices of the lamb shanks, eating *mahicheh* has always been a sensory experience beyond just taste.

4 servings

4 lamb shanks
Salt and pepper to taste
2 tablespoons unsalted butter
1 yellow onion, chopped
8 garlic cloves, minced and crushed into a paste
¼ teaspoon ground turmeric
2 tablespoons saffron water
Water

- Rinse the lamb shanks in running water and pat them dry with paper towels. Sprinkle them with a generous amount of salt and pepper.
- In a large pot or Dutch oven, melt butter over medium-high heat. Place the lamb shanks in the pot and sear them for a few minutes on each side until they are nicely browned.
- Add the onion and garlic to the lamb and cook until the onion turns translucent. Add the turmeric and stir.
- Pour the saffron water and 2 cups of water over the lamb shanks, cover the pot, and simmer over medium-low heat until the meat is very tender and falling off the bone (about 1.5 hours).
- Taste the broth and adjust seasoning as necessary. Serve with Dill Rice with Fava Beans (see recipe on page 168).

Herb-Stuffed Roasted Fish (*Mahi*)

This is traditionally served for Nowruz (Persian New Year), which takes place in March on the first day of spring. The fish symbolizes life and also represents the concurrent event of the sun leaving the zodiac of Pisces.

4 servings

1 medium-sized, whole fish, scaled, gutted and cleaned (halibut, trout, etc.)
1 tablespoon olive oil
Salt and pepper to taste
1 lemon, sliced, plus more for garnish
2 garlic cloves, sliced
1 scallion, chopped
½ cup chopped flat-leaf parsley
½ cup chopped cilantro
½ cup chopped dill
3 tablespoons unsalted butter

- Preheat oven to 450°F.
- Rub the outside of the fish with oil and place it in a foil-lined baking dish. Sprinkle both sides with salt and pepper. Season the internal cavity with salt and pepper, and place the lemon slices, garlic and herbs inside. Slice the butter into 3 equal pieces and place them inside too.
- Arrange the extra lemon slices on top of the fish. If desired, tie the fish closed with kitchen twine. Bake, turning over once, for 15-20 minutes until golden brown. Serve with Mixed Herb Rice (see recipe on page 169).

Jumbo Meat and Rice Meatballs (*Koofteh Berenji*)

Meatballs are a fun dish to make and eat. Studded throughout with herbs and barberries, these meatballs look fancy but are easy to prepare. Feel free to adjust the ingredients to suit your liking; you can add chopped nuts for a little crunch, substitute ground turkey for a leaner option, or add different seasonings. Some people insert extra ingredients in the center of each meatball, such as a peeled boiled egg and/or a piece of dried fruit (like prunes or apricots).

6-8 servings

Meatballs:
1 cup basmati rice, rinsed
½ cup yellow split peas, picked over and rinsed
Water
1 pound ground beef or lamb
1 medium yellow onion, peeled and grated
2 eggs
2 garlic cloves
2 scallions, chopped
½ cup flat-leaf parsley, chopped
2 tablespoons dill, chopped
2 tablespoons dried barberries, rinsed
1 teaspoon ground turmeric
Salt and pepper to taste

Cooking Liquid:
2 cups low-sodium chicken stock
1 tablespoon tomato paste
1 tablespoon freshly squeezed lemon juice

Sauce:
½ cup yogurt
1 tablespoon dill, chopped

- In a large pot, bring 3 cups of water to a boil. Add rice, split peas and a pinch of salt and cook for 15 minutes. Drain and set aside.
- In a large bowl, combine the rice and peas with the rest of the meatball ingredients and knead well to combine. Form the mixture into tennis ball-sized meatballs, cover, and refrigerate for 1 hour (as noted, you may add extra fillings inside the center of each meatball before refrigerating).
- In a large pot, add the chicken stock, tomato paste and lemon juice and cook over medium-high heat, stirring, until the tomato paste is mixed evenly throughout and the stock is heated through.
- Carefully place the meatballs into the stock and reduce the heat to medium-low. Cover and cook for 1 hour until meatballs are tender and cooked through.
- To serve, place the meatballs in a serving dish and pour any remaining stock around them. Mix the yogurt and dill together and drizzle over the top of the meatballs. Serve with salad, yogurt and herbs.

Stuffed Bell Peppers (*Dolmeh Felfel*)

Dolmeh refers to any stuffed vegetables, be they grape leaves, cabbage, potatoes, eggplants or—in this case—bell peppers. Colorful stuffed peppers make an attractive and fun dish that can be used as a side or as the main entrée. You can use this filling to prepare other types of *dolmeh* as well.

4 servings

Water
½ cup basmati rice
4 bell peppers (red, orange or yellow)
2 tablespoons canola oil
1 medium yellow onion
4 garlic cloves, minced
½ pound ground beef, lamb or turkey
Salt and pepper to taste
½ teaspoon ground turmeric
½ teaspoon ground cumin
¼ teaspoon ground cinnamon
2 scallions, chopped
½ cup flat-leaf parsley, chopped
¼ cup mint leaves, chopped (or 1 tablespoon dried mint)
1 tablespoon dried tarragon
2 tablespoons tomato paste, divided
1 tablespoon saffron water

- In a small pot, bring 2 cups of water to a boil. Add the rice and cook until the rice is cooked through (about 15 minutes). Drain and set aside.
- Wash and dry bell peppers. Cut off and save their tops, and scoop out their seeds. Rub a small amount of salt on the inside of each pepper.
- *Optional step:* Grill the peppers, turning them over often, until the skins develop a light char (but don't let the peppers get very soft).

- In a large pan over medium heat, sauté onion and garlic in oil until the onion turns translucent. Add the meat, salt, pepper, turmeric, cumin and cinnamon. Cook until the meat is browned, using a wooden spoon to break the meat up into tiny crumbles while it's cooking. Once the meat is done, add the tomato paste and stir well.
- Turn off the heat. Add the rice and herbs and stir well to combine all of the ingredients.
- Spoon the filling into each pepper and put their tops back on.
- In a large pot, bring 1 cup of water to a boil. Add a pinch of salt, 1 tablespoon of tomato paste, and the saffron water and stir well. Place the peppers inside, cover, and cook for 30 minutes on medium-low heat until the peppers are soft. Serve with salad, yogurt and herbs.

Smoked Eggplant and Tomato Casserole with Garlic and Eggs (*Mirza Ghasemi*)

Eggs add body and substance to this dish, which can be served as an appetizer or as a dip as well as a light vegetarian entrée. Warm pieces of flatbread are traditionally used to scoop it up in place of spoons.

4-6 servings

2 large eggplants
3 eggs
Salt and pepper to taste
¼ cup olive oil
4-6 garlic cloves, minced
1 teaspoon ground turmeric
4 large tomatoes, diced (or 2 [15-ounce] cans diced tomatoes)
1 tablespoon tomato paste
¼ cup water
1 tablespoon chopped chives (or 1 teaspoon dried)
¼ cup chopped walnuts, plus more for garnish (optional)
Salt and pepper to taste

- Place the eggplants on a hot grill over an open flame. Cook, turning occasionally, until they become soft and the skin becomes blistered and blackened. (Alternate method if not using a grill: Preheat oven to 400°F. Prick eggplants all over with a fork. Place them on a baking sheet and roast them in the oven for 30-40 minutes until tender.)
- Remove the eggplants from the grill or oven and let them cool to the touch. Peel away the skins and chop up the flesh. Place the flesh in a bowl and mash it well with a fork. Set aside.
- In a separate bowl, crack the eggs and whisk them together to blend the yolks and the whites. Set aside.
- Heat olive oil over medium heat in a large pan. Add the garlic and cook for about 5 minutes, then add the turmeric and stir.

- Add the eggplants and the rest of the ingredients (minus the eggs) to the pan. Cook on medium-high heat, stirring often, until there is no liquid left.
- Pour the eggs into the mixture and stir until the eggs are cooked through. Remove from heat. Garnish with walnuts.
- Serve with bread, yogurt and fresh herbs.

Persian-Style Spaghetti and Meat Sauce

I like to imagine that the first Iranian to encounter pasta wasn't sure what to do with it, so they decided to treat it as they would treat rice. That is basically the way that Persian spaghetti is prepared. You want to make sure you only parboil the spaghetti before steaming it; otherwise, it will turn mushy. The steaming process makes the meat sauce stick to the pasta and creates a unique texture that I love.

6-8 servings

Water
Salt
1 (16-ounce) box dry spaghetti
1 large yellow onion, diced
1 cup shelled green peas (frozen is fine)
4 garlic cloves, minced
1 teaspoon ground turmeric
4 tablespoons canola oil, divided
1 pound ground beef
1 (6-ounce) can tomato paste
1 (14-ounce) can tomato puree
1 teaspoon dried oregano
Salt and pepper to taste
½ cup chopped flat-leaf parsley

- Bring a pot of water to a boil. Add a pinch of salt plus the spaghetti and boil until the pasta is about halfway done. Drain the spaghetti and set it aside.
- In a large pan, sauté the onion in oil over medium-high heat until golden brown. Add the green peas, garlic, and turmeric. Stir well and cook until the peas have thawed (if using frozen) and begun to soften.
- Add the ground beef and cook until browned. While cooking, use a wooden spoon to break up the ground beef into tiny crumbles.

- Add the tomato paste, puree, 1 cup of water, oregano, salt and pepper. Cover, reduce heat to low, and simmer the sauce for about 30 minutes. A few minutes before it's done, add the parsley and stir.
- In a large, heavy-bottomed pot, add 2 tablespoons of oil. Toss the spaghetti and sauce together and place the mixture into the pot. Cover the top of the pot with a kitchen towel or a fabric lid cover and place the lid on. Cook over low heat for 35 minutes or until the spaghetti is cooked through and the sauce sticks to the pasta.

Sausage and Potato Sandwiches (*Sosis Bandari*)

In Farsi, *bandari* literally means "from the port," referring to the many port cities and towns along Iran's southern coast. My friend Firoozeh introduced me to this simple yet delicious sandwich while we were studying together in graduate school.

2 servings

1 tablespoon canola oil
1 yellow onion, finely diced
½ teaspoon ground turmeric
1 large russet potato, peeled and finely diced
¾ pound smoked kielbasa or your favorite sausage, finely diced (you can also use hot dogs)
2 tablespoons tomato paste
1 teaspoon black pepper
Salt to taste
2 hoagie or sub rolls

- In a large pan, heat oil over medium-high heat and add the onion. Sauté until translucent, then add the turmeric and stir well.
- Add potato and sausage and cook until the sausage is browned and cooked through and the potato is tender.
- Add tomato paste, salt and pepper and stir well. Cook for another 2-3 minutes.
- Toast the rolls and fill them with the sausage filling. Serve with *torshi* and chips.

Fish with Spicy Tamarind Sauce

Inspired by southern Iranian cooking, this is a re-interpretation of *ghalieh mahi*, a fish and tamarind stew.

4 servings

½ cup all-purpose flour
½ teaspoon dried fenugreek leaves
½ teaspoon ground turmeric
½ teaspoon chili powder
Salt and pepper to taste
1 egg
4 fillets of cod, halibut, tilapia or another mild, white-fleshed fish
2 tablespoons unsalted butter
1 tablespoon canola oil
1 shallot, sliced
1 garlic clove, minced
2 tablespoons tamarind pulp
Water
1 tablespoon honey
½ teaspoon red pepper flakes
½ cup chopped cilantro, plus more for garnish

- In a shallow dish, combine the flour, fenugreek, turmeric, chili powder, salt and pepper. In another dish, crack the egg and whisk it together with 1 tablespoon of water.
- Dip each fish fillet in the egg mixture and then in the flour mixture, making sure to get an even coating on both sides.
- Melt the butter in a large pan over medium-high heat. Add the fish fillets and fry them, turning once, until they are cooked through and golden brown on both sides. Place the fish on a serving dish.
- Wipe the inside of the pan with a paper towel and add the oil, shallot and garlic. Cook until shallot turns translucent.
- In the meantime, place the tamarind in a bowl with about ½ cup of warm water. Use your fingers to rub the tamarind pulp until it has dissolved. If there are any solids, strain them out.

- Add the tamarind liquid to the shallot, along with the honey, red pepper flakes, cilantro, salt and pepper. Stir well and reduce the heat to medium-low. Let the sauce simmer until it thickens.
- Pour the sauce over the fish fillets and garnish them with more chopped cilantro. Serve with rice and salad.

Beef Tongue Sandwiches

Many people are reluctant to try tongue, and I understand their apprehension, because I was one of them for many years. My parents would occasionally cook it, and I had to admit that it always smelled delicious, but I couldn't bring myself to eat it. The first time I actually tried tongue was at a Mexican taqueria serving tongue tacos. I was immediately hooked. It is an amazingly tender, melt-in-your-mouth, flavorful piece of meat, owing partly to its high fat content. It doesn't have a particularly strong taste like some other organ meats; it is mild and sweet. It is excellent both hot and cold and makes a great sandwich filling.

4 servings

1 (2-3 pound) beef tongue
8 garlic cloves, crushed
1 bay leaf
Salt and pepper to taste
Water
2 tablespoons unsalted butter
1 pound white mushrooms, sliced
1 yellow onion, sliced
1 large baguette, cut into 4 pieces (or 4 sandwich rolls)
½ cup mayonnaise
1 tablespoon Dijon mustard
16 dill pickle slices

- Rinse the tongue very well under running water. Place it in a large pot on the stove, along with 6 garlic cloves, the bay leaf, salt, pepper, and enough water to just cover the tongue. Cover the pot and turn the heat on to medium-low. Simmer the tongue for 3 hours until the meat is very tender when pierced with a fork. The skin on the tongue will have turned white.
- Remove the tongue from the pot and let it cool for 5 minutes. Then, while it's still hot, peel the skin off of the tongue using a sharp knife and your hands. The cooler the meat gets, the more difficult it is to peel the skin, so work quickly. Once

you've peeled the tongue, slice it and chop it into pieces—again, this is easier while the meat is still hot. Place the chopped tongue in a bowl and set it aside.
- In a large pan, melt the butter over medium-high heat and add the mushrooms, onion and the remaining 2 garlic cloves. Cook until the onion turns golden brown. Season with salt and pepper to taste, and turn off the heat.
- Spread open the baguette pieces or sandwich rolls and toast them in a 170°F oven for 5-8 minutes. Mix together the mayonnaise and mustard and spread this on each piece of bread.
- Arrange dill 4 pickle slices on one half of each baguette. Place tongue meat on the other half and top it with some of the mushroom mixture. Close the sandwich and press down on it firmly. Enjoy!

Iranian-Style Pizza

Pizza delivery places have developed a strong presence in Tehran. The pizzas are baked without sauce—the sauce comes with the pizza in separate packets and is then squeezed on top of the pizza, much like ketchup.

4-6 servings

1 store-bought pizza dough
2 tablespoons olive oil
2 cups shredded mozzarella cheese
4 ounces mortadella, chopped
1 small onion, diced
1 green bell pepper, diced
¼ cup cooked corn kernels
1 teaspoon dried thyme

Sauce:
3 tablespoons tomato paste
⅓ cup water
1 teaspoon honey
½ teaspoon onion powder
½ teaspoon dried oregano
¼ teaspoon dried parsley
Salt and pepper to taste

- Roll out or toss the pizza dough until it's between ⅛ and ¼ an inch thick. Brush the olive oil all over the top of the dough.
- Sprinkle the mozzarella on top of the dough. Arrange mortadella, onion, bell pepper and corn on top of the cheese. Sprinkle thyme over the whole pizza.
- Bake the pizza in the oven according to the directions on the dough's package and the tools you have (baking sheet, pizza stone, etc.). While the pizza is baking, mix all the ingredients for the sauce in a bowl. Stir the sauce well until it's smooth.

- When the pizza is done, remove it from the oven and slice it. While eating, dip each slice into the sauce or spread some sauce on top of the pizza.

Persian-Inspired Nachos

Layers of Persian-spiced meat and beans with herbs, veggies, cheese and a creamy sauce result in these simply outstanding nachos. Serve these at your next party and watch them disappear!

4-6 servings

1 yellow onion, diced
2 garlic cloves, minced
1 tablespoon canola oil
1 teaspoon ground turmeric
½ teaspoon ground cumin
½ teaspoon ground cinnamon
1 pound ground beef or lamb
1 tablespoon dried mint leaves
Salt and pepper to taste
1 (15-ounce) can kidney beans, drained and rinsed
1 large bag tortilla chips
2 cups crumbled feta cheese
1 cup Cucumber, Tomato and Onion Salad (see recipe on page 70)
½ cup Pomegranate Salsa (see recipe on page 201)
2 scallions, chopped
½ cup liquid *kashk*, warmed through
Lime wedges
Hot sauce (optional)

- In a large pan over medium-high heat, sauté onion and garlic in the oil until onion turns golden brown. Add the turmeric, cumin and cinnamon and stir well. Cook for another minute until fragrant.
- Add the meat and cook until it is no longer pink. Use a wooden spoon to break up the meat into tiny crumbles while it cooks.
- Add the mint, salt, pepper and beans to the meat and stir well. Cook for another 3-4 minutes, then remove from heat.
- Arrange a layer of chips in a serving dish. Top with half of the meat and bean mixture as well as half of the feta cheese, salad, salsa, scallions and *kashk*.

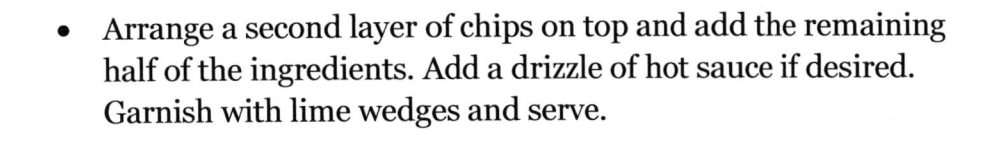

- Arrange a second layer of chips on top and add the remaining half of the ingredients. Add a drizzle of hot sauce if desired. Garnish with lime wedges and serve.

The Persian Muffuletta

The muffuletta is a classic New Orleans sandwich of Italian-American origins; it is known for its round loaf of bread containing olive salad and a stack of deli meats. In this version, I've added feta cheese in place of mozzarella and provolone as well as Persian pickled vegetables in place of the olive salad.

2-4 servings

1 large round loaf of Italian bread
Olive oil
½ cup mixed vegetable *torshi*
¼ cup chopped walnuts
¼ cup chopped dill
4 ounces sliced mortadella
4 ounces sliced Genoa salami
4 ounces sliced ham
½ cup crumbled feta cheese

- Place the loaf of bread on a flat surface. Press one hand on top of it and use the other to slice the loaf in half horizontally with a bread knife. Separate the halves and hollow them out by removing some of the bread in the center.
- Spread each half with olive oil and *torshi*.
- Layer meats, feta, walnuts and dill on each half and put them together. Cut the sandwich into quarters and serve; alternatively, wrap the whole sandwich in plastic wrap and refrigerate for a few hours to allow the flavors to mingle before slicing and serving.

Rice

~*~*~

Mounds of fluffy rice, tinted with saffron and studded with nuts, dried fruits and herbs, is the first image that comes to my mind when I think of Persian food. Rice is a staple in Persian cuisine, and its preparation is akin to an art form. In Iran, many varieties of rice are cultivated in the Gilan province of northern Iran surrounding the Caspian Sea. It is not difficult to make authentic Persian-style rice, but it often requires patience.

Chelow refers to plain rice (or rice tinted with saffron), while polow refers to rice mixed with other ingredients like herbs, vegetables and meat. Sticky rice, which is sometimes eaten at breakfast and is also eaten to settle upset stomachs, is known as kateh.

White Rice with Saffron (Chelow) and Crisp Golden Crust (Tahdig)

"Sweet" Rice with Barberries, Nuts, Carrots and Candied Orange Peel (Shirin Polow)

Tart Cherry Rice (Albaloo Polow)

Dill Rice with Fava Beans (Baghali Polow)

Mixed Herb Rice (Sabzi Polow)

Lentil Rice (Adaas Polow)

Green Bean Rice with Beef (Loobia Polow)

Cabbage Rice with Lamb Meatballs (Kalam Polow)

Chicken, Rice and Yogurt 'Casserole' (Tahchin)

Toasted Mung Bean Rice (Maash Polow)

Apple, Raisin and Garlic Rice

Butternut Squash Rice with Pomegranate and Pumpkin Seeds

Persian Fried Rice

Low-Carb Cauliflower "Rice"

White Rice with Saffron (*Chelow*) and a Crisp Golden Crust (*Tahdig*)

This is a basic rice dish that pairs well with any kind of *khoresht*, kabob or other entrée. All types of rice dishes are basically prepared as a variation on this method. Cooking times will vary depending on your particular equipment, so keep a close eye on the rice until you've perfected your method.

4-6 servings

2 cups basmati rice
6 cups water plus 2 tablespoons
Salt
2-3 tablespoons canola oil
Unsalted butter (optional)
2 tablespoons saffron water

- Rinse the rice under cold running water until the water runs clear. This step removes excess starch from the rice and helps the grains become fluffy and well-defined.
- *Optional step:* Soak the rice in a bowl of water, with a pinch of salt added, for 30 minutes. This is not necessary but will help remove additional starch.
- In a large, heavy-bottomed pot, bring 6 cups of water to a boil. Once it is boiling, add the rice to the pot along with 1 teaspoon of salt.
- Parboil the rice for about 5-10 minutes. The grains should be firm on the inside but soft on the outside. Taste the rice after 5 minutes to see. Cooking times may vary based on your equipment. You don't want the rice to be overcooked at this point, because then it will become mushy after the steaming process. In addition, avoid rigorous stirring while the rice is cooking. Every few minutes, gently stir the rice up from the bottom of the pot and then leave it alone. Over-stirring will break up the rice and make it mushy.

- Place a fine-holed colander in the sink and drain the rice. Rinse the rice with cold water to halt the cooking process (again, avoid handling the rice too much).
- Add the oil to your pot. Then, transfer the parboiled rice back into the pot, using a large spoon or spatula to stack the rice in a pyramidal shape. When you're done, poke 3-4 deep holes in the rice pyramid with the end of a wooden spoon to allow steam to escape during the next part of the process.
- Wrap the lid of the pot in a kitchen towel, or place a fabric lid cover on top of the pot, and place the lid on. Turn the heat to its lowest setting and let the rice cook for 45 minutes to 1 hour until the rice is fluffy and completely cooked through. Transfer the rice to a serving platter. Reserve one cup of the rice and mix it with the saffron water until it turns completely yellow. Layer the yellow rice on top of the rest of the rice and serve. If desired, pour melted butter on top.

Tahdig

Tahdig (which translates as "bottom of the pot") is a layer of deliciously crunchy, golden rice that forms on the bottom of the pot of rice during cooking. Its satisfying texture makes it a popular addition to a meal and it always disappears quickly from any Persian table. Let's face it, not many people dislike things that are crispy and fried!

Making *tahdig* takes practice. You will inevitably end up with too-soft *tahdig* as well as burned-to-a-crisp *tahdig* at some point. As long as you add plenty of oil to the bottom of the pot, it is easier to avoid burning it. The result should always be crisp and golden brown.

Serving Tahdig

Method 1 (the pretty and professional method):

Hold a large serving platter firmly against the top of the pot of rice and quickly turn the pot and platter over together. Let gravity do its work, and gently shake them up and down to help dislodge the rice and *tahdig*. You should end up with a round "cake" of rice topped with a golden *tahdig* crust. Cut it like a cake for an attractive presentation.

Note: If necessary, you can wrap the bottom of the pot with a damp towel for a few minutes first to help loosen the crust.

Method 2 (the arm workout method):

First, dish all of the rice out onto the platter and then use a sturdy metal spatula to scrape the *tahdig* out of the pot in large pieces. Serve them plain or with *khoresht* ladled on top.

Tahdig Recipes

Basic Rice *Tahdig*

Follow the recipe for White Rice with Saffron (see recipe on page 160). Before you add the parboiled rice back into the pot to finish cooking, add enough canola oil, vegetable oil or clarified butter (ghee) to the pot to form a ¼-inch thick layer that evenly covers the bottom. Then, add 2 tablespoons of saffron water to the pot before adding the parboiled rice. Continue to steam the rice over low heat for 45 minutes to 1 hour as instructed. The *tahdig* will form at the bottom of the pot while the rice is steaming, and the saffron will help enrich its golden hue.

Variation: To give the *tahdig* some extra flavor, mix 1 cup of the parboiled rice with 1 cup of yogurt and 2 tablespoons of saffron water. Add the oil or ghee and then add this mixture to the bottom of the pot before adding the rest of the parboiled rice. This technique also works with all types of *tahdig* listed below.

Potato Tahdig

Follow the recipe for Basic Rice *Tahdig*, but after adding the oil or ghee, peel and slice a medium-sized potato into ¼ inch thick slices and arrange them in a single layer on the bottom of the pot. Finish as instructed. For a fun variation, use a cookie cutter to cut the potato slices into shapes first.

Lettuce Tahdig

Follow the recipe for Basic Rice *Tahdig*, but after adding the oil or ghee, wash and dry leaves of romaine lettuce. Arrange the leaves in a single layer on the bottom of the pot. Finish as instructed.

Flatbread Tahdig

Follow the recipe for Basic Rice *Tahdig*, but after adding the oil or ghee, arrange pieces of lavash bread in a single layer on the bottom of the pot. Finish as instructed.

A Note on Brown Rice

Brown basmati rice can be used in place of white rice for any Persian rice recipe. Follow all of the same steps as you would in making white basmati rice: rinse and soak the rice, parboil, drain and steam. Brown rice generally requires more water and a longer cooking time than white rice, so keep an eye on the rice while it is steaming. If necessary, add water as needed (½ cup at a time) to the brown rice while it steams to prevent it from getting too dry before it fully cooks.

"Sweet" Rice with Barberries, Nuts, Carrots and Candied Orange Peel (*Shirin Polow*)

This delectable rice is served on many special occasions including weddings. Despite being called 'sweet' rice, this dish is actually full of different flavors: tartness from the barberries, nuttiness from the almonds and pistachios, flowery saffron, rich butter...now I'm getting hungry!

4-6 servings

¾ cup dried barberries
Water
⅓ cup slivered almonds
⅓ cup chopped pistachios
2 tablespoons unsalted butter, divided
2 cups julienned or 'matchstick' carrots
2 tablespoons granulated sugar, divided
2 tablespoons orange zest
½ teaspoon ground cinnamon
½ teaspoon ground cumin
¼ teaspoon salt
White Rice with Saffron (*Chelow*) (see recipe on page 160)

- Soak the dried barberries in about 1 cup of water for 20 minutes and then drain them.
- Place a large pan on the stove, turn the heat on to low, and add almonds and pistachios. Toast them, with no added grease, until you can start to smell their aroma. Pour them in a separate, large mixing bowl and set aside.
- Melt 1 tablespoon of butter in the pan over medium-high heat and add the carrots. Sauté for about 5 minutes until the carrots soften. Add 1 tablespoon of the sugar, plus the orange zest, cinnamon, cumin and salt. Stir well and turn the heat down to low. Cook for another 4-5 minutes and then add the mixture to the almonds and pistachios.

- Wipe the pan with a paper towel and melt another tablespoon of butter over low heat. Add the barberries and 1 tablespoon sugar and cook, stirring, for 2-3 minutes. Add the barberries to the nut and carrot mixture and stir it well.
- Mix a few spoonfuls of the barberry and carrot mixture with the saffron-tinted yellow rice you made following the *Chelow* recipe. On a serving platter, arrange alternating layers of white rice and the barberry and carrot mixture, topping it all off with the yellow rice mixed with the barberries and carrots. Serve with your choice of kabobs or *khoresht*, yogurt, salad and herbs.

Tart Cherry Rice (*Albaloo Polow*)

I love how festive this rice looks, with its plump pinkish cherries embedded throughout. The tartness and sweetness combined with the aroma of saffron and butter is intoxicating. A common variation on this dish is to prepare tiny beef or lamb meatballs (about ½-inch wide) and mix them with the cherry rice.

4-6 servings

White Rice with Saffron (*Chelow*) (see recipe on page 160)
4 cups pitted tart cherries
¼ cup granulated sugar
4 tablespoons unsalted butter, melted
2 tablespoons saffron water

- *If using fresh or frozen tart cherries:* Thaw the cherries if they're frozen. In a large saucepan, combine the cherries and sugar. Cover and simmer over medium-low heat for 15-20 minutes until cherries have softened and sugar has melted. Drain the cherries, reserving the syrup, and set them aside. Return the syrup to the saucepan and let it reduce by simmering over low heat for about 10 minutes. Set aside.
- *If using jarred tart cherries:* If the cherries are in syrup, drain them and reserve the syrup. If the syrup is thin, you may want to heat it with sugar in a saucepan until the sugar dissolves and the syrup thickens.
- Follow the recipe for White Rice with Saffron (*Chelow*), but when it's time to add the parboiled rice back into the pot to steam, create alternating layers of rice and cherries. Pour the melted butter and the saffron water over the rice before steaming. Finish cooking the rice as instructed. When the rice is done, pour about ½ cup of the reserved syrup over the rice. Serve with your choice of meat or *khoresht*, yogurt, salad and herbs.

Dill Rice with Fava Beans (*Baghali Polow*)

The fresh taste of dill and fava beans in this dish makes me think of spring. This rice is traditionally served with lamb shanks. You can substitute lima beans if you don't have fava beans and it will be just as delicious. You can also use dried dill instead of fresh dill if that's what you have on hand, but try to use fresh if you can—it makes a big difference in flavor.

4-6 servings

1 teaspoon olive oil
1 garlic clove, minced
1 pound fava or broad beans, peeled
Salt to taste
White Rice with Saffron (*Chelow*) (see recipe on page 160)
3 cups fresh dill, finely chopped (or use 1 cup of dried dill)
2 tablespoons saffron water
2 tablespoons unsalted butter, melted (optional)

- In a pan, heat olive oil over medium heat and add garlic and beans. Sauté beans until they are just cooked through, about 5 minutes. Season with salt.
- Follow the recipe for White Rice with Saffron (*Chelow*), and as you are adding the parboiled rice back into the pot to steam, create alternating layers of rice, dill, and beans. Drizzle the saffron water and melted butter over the rice and finish cooking as instructed.
- Serve with Braised Lamb Shanks in Garlic Broth (*Mahicheh*) (see recipe on page 139).

Mixed Herb Rice (*Sabzi Polow*)

This rice truly showcases the Iranian love of herbs. If you grow your own herbs, this recipe is a great way to use them. Feel free to use whichever herbs you like the best. *Sabzi polow* is often served with fish—in fact, this combination is a traditional meal for Persian New Year (see Herb-Stuffed Roasted Fish recipe).

4-6 servings

1 cup dill, chopped
1 cup flat-leaf parsley, chopped
1 cup cilantro, chopped
1 cup scallions, chopped (green parts only)
White Rice with Saffron (*Chelow*) (see recipe on page 160)
2 tablespoons saffron water
2 tablespoons unsalted butter, melted (optional)

- In a large bowl, combine the herbs and scallions.
- Fellow the recipe for White Rice with Saffron (*Chelow*). While adding the parboiled rice back into the pot to steam, create alternating layers of rice and herbs. Drizzle the saffron water and butter over the rice and finish cooking as instructed.
- Serve with Herb-Stuffed Roasted Fish (see recipe on page 140).

Lentil Rice (*Adaas Polow*)

The contrast between the earthy richness of the lentils and the sweetness of the dates and raisins makes this rice totally addictive.

4-6 servings

2 tablespoons unsalted butter
1 shallot, diced
½ cup pitted dates, chopped
½ cup raisins
¼ teaspoon ground cinnamon
¼ teaspoon ground cumin
¼ teaspoon ground turmeric
White Rice with Saffron (*Chelow*) (see recipe on page 160)
2 cups dried green or brown lentils, picked over and rinsed
3 cups water
1 teaspoon salt
2 tablespoons saffron water
2 tablespoons unsalted butter, melted (optional)

- In a pan, sauté shallot in butter over medium heat until translucent. Add dates, raisins, cinnamon, cumin and turmeric and cook, stirring, for another 2-3 minutes. Set aside.
- Put the lentils in a pot and add 3 cups of water. Bring to a boil, then add salt and reduce heat to medium-low. Cook for another 20-25 minutes until lentils are tender. Remove from heat.
- Follow the recipe for White Rice with Saffron (*Chelow*). While adding the parboiled rice back into the pot to steam, create alternating layers of rice, lentils and the raisin mixture. Drizzle the saffron water and butter over the rice and finish cooking as instructed. Serve with your choice of meat or *khoresht*, yogurt, salad and herbs; or, serve the rice as a vegetarian entrée.

Green Bean Rice with Beef (*Loobia Polow*)

I love this hearty combination of green beans with beef in tomato-infused rice. It's like an entire dinner in one rice dish. Traditionally, this dish is not spicy, but I love the way it tastes with the addition of extra pepper and/or hot sauce. If you enjoy spicy food, then I recommend making this one spicy.

4-6 servings

1 tablespoon olive oil
1 small yellow onion, diced
2 garlic cloves, minced
½ teaspoon ground turmeric
1 pound ground beef (or beef stewing meat cut into ½-inch pieces)
1 pound fresh green beans, ends and strings removed, cut into 1-inch pieces (frozen is fine too)
1 large tomato, diced
1 (16-ounce) can tomato puree
¼ cup fresh squeezed lime juice
¼ cup hot sauce (optional)
Salt and pepper to taste
½ teaspoon ground cinnamon
White Rice with Saffron (*Chelow*) (see recipe on page 160)
2 tablespoons saffron water
2 tablespoons unsalted butter, melted

- In a pan, sauté onion and garlic in olive oil over medium-high heat until onion is translucent. Add the turmeric and stir. Add beef and cook until it is thoroughly browned. If using ground beef, use a wooden spoon to break it up into tiny crumbles as it cooks.

- Add green beans, tomato, tomato puree, lime juice, hot sauce, salt, pepper and cinnamon to the pan and stir. Reduce heat to low, cover the pan, and allow the meat and beans to cook for another 15 minutes.

- Follow the recipe for White Rice with Saffron (*Chelow*). While adding the parboiled rice back to the pot to steam, create alternating layers of rice and the beef and green bean mixture. Drizzle saffron water and melted butter over the rice and finish cooking as instructed.
- Serve with yogurt, salad and herbs.

Cabbage Rice with Lamb Meatballs (*Kalam Polow*)

The cabbage in this dish develops an almost buttery flavor which complements the lamb meatballs quite well.

4-6 servings

1 yellow onion, grated
1 pound ground lamb
Salt and pepper to taste
2 tablespoons canola oil, divided
1 medium head of cabbage, shredded (about 8 cups)
1 tablespoon apple cider vinegar
1 teaspoon ground turmeric
½ teaspoon ground cinnamon
½ teaspoon ground cumin
1 tablespoon tomato paste
½ cup warm water
White Rice with Saffron (*Chelow*) (see recipe on page 160)
2 tablespoons saffron water
2 tablespoons unsalted butter, melted (optional)

- In a large bowl, combine the onion, lamb, salt and pepper. Using your hands, create small (½- to ¾-inch in diameter) meatballs.
- Heat 1 tablespoon of oil in a large pan over medium-high heat. Add the meatballs and cook until they are cooked through (about 10 minutes), stirring every few minutes so they brown on all sides. Remove the meatballs from the pan and place them on paper towels to drain any excess oil.
- Add another tablespoon of oil to the pan, and then add the cabbage, vinegar, salt, pepper, turmeric, cinnamon and cumin. Sauté the cabbage until soft. In a mixing bowl, mix together the tomato paste and warm water until smooth. Pour over the cabbage and cook, stirring, for 2-3 minutes. Remove from heat.

- Follow the recipe for White Rice with Saffron (*Chelow*). While adding the parboiled rice back into the pot to steam, create alternating layers of rice, cabbage and meatballs. Drizzle saffron water and melted butter over the rice and finish cooking as instructed.
- Serve with yogurt, salad and herbs.

Chicken, Rice and Yogurt 'Casserole' (*Tahchin*)

Taking a bite of hot *tahchin* (which translates as "arranging on the bottom" since the meat ends up on the bottom of the dish) is very satisfying, from the crunch of its crust to the tangy and slightly creamy yogurt-flavored rice. You could definitely try this with beef, lamb or even turkey instead of chicken, and some people even put vegetables in their *tahchin*. The recipe below is for a traditional version with chicken. Simple and rustic, *tahchin* looks very impressive when served but isn't too complicated to make.

6-8 servings

1 pound boneless, skinless chicken breasts or thighs
1 medium yellow onion, peeled and chopped
Salt and pepper to taste
½ teaspoon ground turmeric
Water
2 ½ cups basmati rice
1 ½ cups yogurt
3 egg yolks
2 tablespoons saffron water
1 teaspoon ground cumin
3 tablespoons canola oil

- In a large pot or Dutch oven, combine the chicken, onion, salt, pepper, turmeric, and 1 cup of water. Cover and bring to a boil, then reduce the heat to medium-low and simmer for about an hour until the chicken is cooked through and tender. Let the chicken cool and then cut or shred it into bite-sized pieces. Set aside.
- In the meantime, bring 6 cups of water to a boil in a separate pot. Add the rice and a heavy pinch of salt. Parboil the rice until it is tender on the outside but hard on the inside (about 7-10 minutes). Drain the rice and set it aside.
- In a mixing bowl, combine the yogurt, egg yolks, saffron water, cumin, and salt and pepper to taste. Add 2 cups of the parboiled rice and stir well to combine the rice and yogurt.

- Grease the bottom of a heavy-bottomed pot or Dutch oven with the oil. Spoon about ⅔ of the rice and yogurt mixture into the pot and flatten it out with your hand, forming an even layer. Add the cooked chicken in an even layer on top. Spoon the remaining rice and yogurt mixture over the chicken. Add the rest of the plain parboiled rice on top and use your hand to gently press it down until the top is flattened.
- Cover and cook over medium-high heat until you can see steam rising from the pot. At that point, remove the lid, place a kitchen towel or a fabric lid cover over the pot, put the lid back on and reduce the heat to low. Let it cook for 1 hour. Remove *tahchin* from heat and let it cool for 15 minutes. Carefully overturn the pot onto a large round serving tray. The rice on the bottom of the pot should have formed a solid crust. Serve *tahchin* with *torshi*, yogurt and mixed herbs.

Toasted Mung Bean Rice (*Maash Polow*)

Not everyone toasts the mung beans for this dish, but I recommend it as it makes a big difference in the flavor.

6-8 servings

White Rice with Saffron (*Chelow*) (see recipe on page 160)
2 cups dried mung beans, picked over, rinsed and dried completely
4 cups water
1 tablespoon canola oil
1 large yellow onion, diced
½ teaspoon ground turmeric
½ teaspoon ground cumin
2 teaspoons salt
1 cup chopped cilantro
2 tablespoons saffron water
2 tablespoons unsalted butter, melted (optional)

- In a medium-sized pot or saucepan, add the mung beans and toast them over medium heat, stirring often, until fragrant. Add 4 cups of water. Cover and bring to a boil, then reduce heat to medium-low and cook for 30-45 minutes or until the beans are tender. Drain and set aside.

- In a pan, sauté the onion in oil over medium heat until caramelized and golden brown. Add turmeric, cumin and salt and stir to combine. Add mung beans and cook, stirring, for an additional 5 minutes. Add the cilantro and stir.

- Follow the recipe for White Rice with Saffron (*Chelow*). While adding the parboiled rice back into the pot to steam, create alternating layers of rice and the mung bean mixture. Drizzle saffron water and melted butter over the rice and finish cooking as instructed.

- Serve with your choice of meat or *khoresht*, yogurt, salad and herbs.

Apple, Raisin and Garlic Rice

This sweet and garlicky rice is inspired by a similar pasta dish of my mom's that has become a Thanksgiving staple for us.

4-6 servings

2 tablespoons olive oil
4 tablespoons unsalted butter, divided
8 garlic cloves, minced
3 Granny Smith apples, peeled, cored and diced
Zest and juice of 1 lemon
Salt and pepper to taste
½ cup raisins
White Rice with Saffron (*Chelow*) (see recipe on page 160)
2 tablespoons saffron water

- In a pan over medium heat, melt 2 tablespoons of butter together with the olive oil. Add the minced garlic and cook for about 5 minutes until the oil is infused with the taste and smell of garlic.
- Add the diced apples, lemon zest and juice, salt and pepper to taste. Sauté until the apples soften, about 6-8 minutes. Add the raisins and sauté for another 2-3 minutes, stirring often.
- Follow the recipe for White Rice with Saffron (*Chelow*), and as you are adding the parboiled rice back into the pot to steam, create alternating layers of rice and apple/raisin mixture. Drizzle the saffron water and the remaining melted butter over the rice and finish cooking as instructed. Serve with your choice of entrée.

Butternut Squash Rice with Pomegranate and Pumpkin Seeds

4-6 servings

1 medium butternut squash
2 tablespoons olive oil
1 teaspoon salt
1 teaspoon black pepper
1 cup pumpkin seeds (pepitas)
1 cup pomegranate seeds
White Rice with Saffron (*Chelow*) (see recipe on page 160)
2 tablespoons saffron water
2 tablespoons unsalted butter, melted

- Preheat oven to 400°F.
- Peel the squash and slice it in half lengthwise. Remove the guts and seeds and cut the remaining flesh into 1-inch cubes. Toss them with olive oil, salt and pepper and spread them out in a single layer on a baking sheet. Roast them in the oven for 30 minutes until tender.
- In a dry pan over medium heat, toast the pumpkin seeds until fragrant.
- Follow the recipe for White Rice with Saffron (*Chelow*), and as you are adding the parboiled rice back into the pot to steam, create alternating layers of rice, butternut squash and pumpkin seeds. Drizzle the saffron water and the melted butter over the rice and finish cooking as instructed. When the rice is done, add the pomegranate seeds and stir gently to combine all of the ingredients. Serve with your choice of entrée.

Persian Fried Rice

There's usually plenty of leftover rice in a Persian kitchen. What better way to use up leftover rice than making fried rice?

4 servings

2 tablespoons unsalted butter
1 yellow onion, diced
1 garlic clove, minced
½ teaspoon ground turmeric
½ teaspoon ground cumin
¼ teaspoon ground cinnamon
½ cup shelled green peas
½ cup diced carrots
¼ cup raisins
¼ cup slivered almonds
3 cups cooked basmati rice
3 eggs
1 tablespoon saffron water
Salt and pepper to taste

- Melt butter in a medium-sized pot or saucepan over medium heat. Add onion and sauté until caramelized and golden brown. Add garlic and cook for another 2-3 minutes. Add turmeric, cumin and cinnamon and stir well.
- Add peas and carrots and cook for 5-7 minutes until softened.
- Add raisins and almonds and cook for another 2-3 minutes.
- Add rice and stir well.
- Crack the eggs into a separate bowl and whisk them together. Add the saffron water. Pour this mixture over the rice and cook, stirring, until the eggs are cooked through.
- Season with salt and pepper and stir well. Remove from heat and serve.

Low-Carb Cauliflower "Rice"

If you're looking for a way to cut back on carbohydrates then this recipe is a great one to have in your bag of culinary tricks. This recipe is for a basic rice flavored with shallots and garlic, but you can season the cauliflower however you like for more variety.

4-6 servings

1 cauliflower head
2 tablespoons canola oil or unsalted butter
1 shallot, diced
2 garlic cloves, minced
Salt and pepper to taste

- Roughly chop the cauliflower into pieces and place them in a food processor. Pulse until they form crumbles that are each roughly the size of a grain of rice.
- In a pan, heat the oil or butter over medium heat. Add the shallot and garlic and sauté until the shallot turns translucent.
- Add the cauliflower crumbles and sauté for 5-6 minutes until they soften. Serve as you would regular rice.

Sides and Snacks

~*~*~

Fresh Vegetable and Herb Platter (Sabzi Khordan)

Yogurt with Cucumber (Maast o Khiar)

Yogurt with Spinach and Garlic (Borani Esfenaj)

Yogurt with Eggplant (Borani Bademjan)

Yogurt with Persian Shallots (Maast o Musir)

Persian-Spiced Beans (Loobia Pokhteh)

Stuffed Grape Leaves (Dolmeh Barg-e Mo)

Beef and Potato Patties (Kotlet)

Creamy Fried Eggplant Dip (Kashk-e Bademjan)

Olives with Pomegranate and Walnuts (Zeytoon Parvardeh)

Persian-Spiced Fried Potatoes

Minced Lamb Pastries

Zesty Corn in Lime and Butter

Sautéed Kale and White Beans with Fenugreek

Barberry and Dill Cornbread

Pomegranate Salsa

Fresh Vegetable and Herb Platter (*Sabzi Khordan*)

Fresh herbs are traditionally eaten alongside a Persian meal. The flavors perfectly complement the aromas and flavors of traditional Persian foods. It's not always necessary to have *sabzi khordan* at the table, but it's definitely a nice touch, especially if you're serving guests. Below is a list of ingredients that you can arrange on a platter of your own. Modify this list to suit your own tastes.

6-12 servings

Mint
Parsley
Basil
Tarragon
Cilantro
Chives
Scallions
Radishes
Onions
Walnut halves, soaked overnight in salt water
Olives
Feta cheese, cut into cubes
Butter, cut into slices
Persian flatbread (lavash, taftoon, barbari, or sangak) or pita bread

YOGURT DISHES

Yogurt is at the table, in some form, at almost every Persian meal. It is believed to have multiple health benefits including aiding in digestion. Some of the tastiest Persian side dishes are prepared simply by mixing fresh ingredients with yogurt. In addition to being served as sides, these yogurt dishes can also serve as the focal point of a light meal. Sometimes all I need is a big bowl of *maast o khiar* (yogurt with cucumber) and a few pieces of warm bread, and I'm good to go as far as lunch is concerned. Yogurt dishes can also function as dips for chips and veggies.

Yogurt with Cucumber (*Maast o Khiar*)

This dish is a cool and refreshing classic. You can make it with or without the walnuts and raisins. With them, however, this dish perfectly represents the traditional idea of balancing foods that have hot and cold energies (cucumbers and mint are considered cold, while walnuts and raisins are considered hot).

4-8 servings

4 cups yogurt
2 medium cucumbers, peeled, seeds removed, grated
2 tablespoons dried mint leaves
¼ cup chopped walnuts
¼ cup raisins
Salt and pepper to taste
Dried crushed rose petals for garnish (optional)

- Mix all ingredients together in a large bowl. Taste and adjust seasoning as needed.
- Garnish with dried rose petals. Serve, or cover and refrigerate for at least 1 hour before serving to allow flavors to combine.

Yogurt with Spinach and Garlic (*Borani Esfenaj*)

Here's a really quick and tasty way to eat more spinach. You'll be pleasantly surprised at how much flavor lies in such a simple dish.

4-8 servings

1 (10-ounce) package frozen chopped spinach, thawed
3-4 garlic cloves, minced
2 tablespoons olive oil
4 cups yogurt
Salt and pepper to taste

- In a pan over medium heat, cook spinach and garlic in oil until the spinach is completely warmed through and fragrant with garlic.
- In a large bowl, mix together the spinach and garlic with yogurt, salt and pepper. Stir well to combine. Taste and adjust seasoning if needed. Cover and refrigerate for at least 2 hours before serving.

Yogurt with Eggplant (*Borani Bademjan*)

The creaminess of both the eggplant and the yogurt complement each other perfectly in this easy yet flavorful dish.

4-8 servings

1 large eggplant
1 yellow onion, diced
2-3 garlic cloves, minced
2 tablespoons olive oil
1 tablespoon freshly squeezed lemon juice
1 tablespoon dried mint leaves
¼ teaspoon ground turmeric
4 cups yogurt
Salt and pepper to taste
Mint leaves for garnish (optional)

- Preheat oven to 400°F.
- Prick the eggplant all over with a fork. Place it on a baking sheet and roast it in the oven for 40 minutes until soft. Remove it from the oven and let it cool to the touch. Peel away the skin and chop the flesh.
- In a pan, sauté the onion and garlic in olive oil over medium-high heat until onion turns translucent. Add the eggplant, lemon juice, dried mint and turmeric and stir well. Cook for another 2-3 minutes and remove from heat.
- In a large bowl, combine the eggplant mixture with the yogurt, salt and pepper. Stir well. Garnish with chopped fresh mint leaves. Cover and refrigerate for at least 2 hours before serving.

Yogurt with Persian Shallots (*Maast o Musir*)

This is probably the easiest recipe in this book, and it's a great one to know. Use *maast o musir* as a dip, an appetizer or a sauce—it really becomes quite addictive and packs a surprising amount of flavor. You might be tempted to use regular shallots in this dish, but don't—use the Persian variety instead as they have a much more garlicky flavor as opposed to the onion taste of regular shallots.

4 servings

4 cups yogurt
12 slices dried *musir* (Persian shallot)
Salt and pepper to taste

- Soak *musir* in water for 2 hours. Drain, dry and mince it.
- In a bowl, mix together the *musir* and yogurt. Add salt and pepper and stir well.
- Cover and refrigerate for at least 2 hours before serving.

Persian-Spiced Beans (*Loobia Pokhteh*)

Serve these tasty beans with some nice crusty bread, as a side to hot dogs, or even at breakfast with fried eggs.

Variation: If you decide to use canned beans, make sure to drain and rinse them, and add all of the seasonings to the beans at the beginning of cooking. Bring to a boil, then reduce heat and simmer for 15 minutes.

4-6 servings

2 cups dried pinto beans
Water
1 yellow onion, diced
1 tablespoon tomato paste
1 teaspoon *golpar* powder
1 teaspoon ground sumac
½ teaspoon ground turmeric
Juice and zest of ½ a lemon
Salt and pepper to taste
Extra-virgin olive oil

- Place the beans in a bowl and cover them with water. Let them soak for 8 hours or overnight.
- Drain and rinse the beans and place them in a large pot along with the diced onion. Add enough water to cover the beans by 2 inches. Cover and bring to a boil over high heat, then reduce the heat and simmer until the beans are tender, about 1-1.5 hours.
- Add the tomato paste, turmeric, *golpar*, sumac, lemon juice and zest, salt and pepper to the pot and stir well to combine. Simmer for an additional 10-15 minutes. Remove from heat. To serve, ladle in a bowl and drizzle some olive oil on top. You can also sprinkle extra sumac and *golpar* on top if desired.

Stuffed Grape Leaves (*Dolmeh Barg-e Mo*)

Stuffed grape leaves make an impressive and fun-to-eat appetizer, snack or side dish.

Makes approx. 60 dolmeh

2 yellow onions, diced
2 tablespoons canola oil plus 1 tablespoon
2 garlic cloves, minced
½ pound ground beef or lamb
Salt and pepper to taste
¼ teaspoon ground cinnamon
2 cups mint leaves, chopped
2 cups flat-leaf parsley, chopped
1 cup chives, chopped
1 tablespoon dried tarragon
¾ cup cooked basmati rice
2 tablespoons tomato paste
1 teaspoon granulated sugar
Water
1 jar grape leaves in brine
¼ cup freshly squeezed lemon juice

- In a large pan, sauté onions in 2 tablespoons of oil over medium-high heat until golden brown.
- Add garlic, meat, salt, pepper, and cinnamon and continue cooking until the meat is browned. Use a wooden spoon to break up the meat into tiny crumbles while it cooks.
- Add mint, parsley, chives, tarragon, and rice and stir well. Cook for another 3-5 minutes.
- Combine tomato paste with sugar and 3-4 tablespoons of hot water and stir until smooth. Add this to the meat mixture and cook, stirring often, for another 5-7 minutes until the liquid has evaporated. Remove from heat and set aside.
- Remove grape leaves from their jar and rinse them in running water to remove the brine.

- Grease the bottom and sides of a deep glass baking dish with 1 tablespoon of oil. Arrange a few grape leaves across the bottom of the baking dish, ensuring that the entire surface is covered.
- Working on a flat surface, assemble each *dolmeh*. Lay a grape leaf flat and place 1 tablespoon of the filling in its center. If the leaf has a stem, trim it off with kitchen scissors. Starting with the sides, wrap the leaf around the filling, making a tight roll like a little burrito.
- When all the *dolmeh* have been wrapped up snugly, place them (seam sides down) inside the baking dish. The more closely packed they are, the better, as this will help keep them from falling apart during baking.
- Preheat oven to 350°F.
- Mix the lemon juice with ¾ cup of water and a pinch of salt and pour this over the *dolmeh*. Cover the dish with aluminum foil and bake the *dolmeh* for an hour and a half. Remove the foil and add another ½ cup of water mixed with a pinch of salt. Bake for an additional 30 minutes.

Beef and Potato Patties (*Kotlet*)

Kotlet is a meat patty usually made of ground beef and potatoes. These are the ultimate Persian picnic food, delicious hot or cold. I love them cold in sandwiches.

Shaami is a similar dish made with the addition of chickpea flour, which gives the patty a nice crispness and a falafel-like flavor. In this recipe I have added chickpea flour, but you can make it without it.

6-8 servings

1 pound ground beef
1 large russet potato or 2 medium potatoes, peeled and grated
1 large onion, grated
2 eggs
1 tablespoon chickpea flour (optional)
1 teaspoon ground turmeric
Salt and pepper to taste
3 tablespoons canola oil

- In a large mixing bowl, combine all ingredients except for the oil. Using your hands, knead the mixture until well combined. Form the mixture into golf ball-sized meatballs and flatten them into round or oval patties about ¼ to ½ an inch thick.
- Heat 3 tablespoons of oil in a large pan over medium-high heat. Fry the patties until they are cooked through and browned on both sides, turning them over halfway through. Serve warm or cold.

Creamy Fried Eggplant Dip (*Kashk-e Bademjan*)

This mouthwatering spread is rich, creamy, garlicky and absolutely heavenly.

4-6 servings

2 large eggplants
2 large yellow onions, sliced thinly
½ teaspoon ground turmeric
⅓ cup canola oil
6-8 garlic cloves, minced
2 tablespoons dried mint
1 teaspoon saffron water
Salt and pepper to taste
1 cup liquid *kashk*, brought to room temperature

- Preheat oven to 350°F.
- Prick the eggplants all over with a fork. Place them on a baking sheet and roast them for 40 minutes until they become soft. Remove them from the oven and let them cool to the touch. Peel away their skins and mash the flesh in a large mixing bowl with a fork or potato masher.
- In a pan, heat the oil over medium-high heat. Add the onion and sauté, stirring every 5 minutes or so, until they caramelize and turn a deep golden brown. Add the turmeric and stir well. Add the garlic and mint and sauté for 4-5 minutes. Stir this mixture well. Remove about ¼ cup of this mixture and set it aside; this will be used as a garnish for the final dish.
- Add the mashed eggplants, saffron water, salt and pepper to the pan and stir well. Cover and cook over medium-low heat for 15 minutes.
- Add the *kashk*. Reduce heat to low and cook, stirring often, for another 5-6 minutes. Taste and adjust seasoning and amount of *kashk* as needed to maintain a creamy consistency.
- Spoon the *kashk-e bademjan* into a serving dish and top with the reserved onion mixture and a drizzle of *kashk*. Serve with warm bread for dipping.

Olives with Pomegranate and Walnuts (*Zeytoon Parvardeh*)

I first encountered this snack as an appetizer at a dinner party held by a family friend, and I immediately fell in love with both the way it looks and its bold flavors. This dish is originally from Iran's northern Gilan province.

The traditional preparation method leaves the olives whole, but you can also make it similar to a tapenade by first blending the olives in a food processor with the walnuts and garlic.

6-8 servings

3 cups pitted green olives
1 cup pomegranate seeds
1 cup chopped walnuts
4 garlic cloves, minced
½ cup chopped fresh mint leaves (or 2 tablespoons dried)

Dressing:
¼ cup pomegranate syrup
¼ cup olive oil
1 teaspoon *golpar* powder
Salt and pepper to taste

- Use a food processor to pulse the walnuts and garlic together until the walnuts are in small crumbles. Place them in a bowl and add the olives, pomegranate seeds and mint.
- In a bowl, whisk together the dressing ingredients. Pour over the other ingredients and stir well to combine.
- To serve cold, refrigerate for 2 hours before serving. It can also be served at room temperature. Serve with crackers, cheese, herbs and your favorite hors d'oeuvres.

Persian-Spiced Fried Potatoes

Fried potatoes are always a crowd-pleaser. Try these by themselves or alongside your favorite sandwich or omelet.

4-6 servings

6 medium red potatoes
Water
3 tablespoons canola oil
1 red onion, diced
3 garlic cloves, minced
1 teaspoon ground paprika
1 teaspoon ground turmeric
½ teaspoon ground cumin
¼ teaspoon ground cinnamon
Salt and pepper to taste
2 tablespoons chopped cilantro
2 tablespoons chopped chives
1 teaspoon nigella seeds
¼ teaspoon *golpar* powder
Yogurt or liquid *kashk*

- Boil the potatoes in salted water until they are just tender enough to be pierced with a fork. Drain the potatoes and let them cool completely, then dice them into rough 1-inch cubes.
- In a large pan over medium-high heat, heat the oil. Add the onion and sauté until caramelized. Add the garlic, paprika, turmeric, cumin, cinnamon, salt and pepper and stir; cook for another 1 minute. Add the potatoes and stir well. Cook until the potatoes are tender and nicely browned, about 10-15 minutes.
- Add the herbs, nigella seeds and *golpar* to the potatoes and stir well. Serve on a platter and drizzle with yogurt or *kashk*.

Minced Lamb Pastries

These elegant, savory pastries are brimming with flavor. If desired, you can prepare the unbaked pastries in advance, wrap them in plastic and freeze them for a month before using.

Makes 4 pastries

Dough:
1 ¼ cups all-purpose flour, plus more for sprinkling on work surface
½ teaspoon salt
1 stick unsalted butter, chilled and diced
¼ cup ice water
1 egg, beaten (for egg wash)

Filling:
½ pound ground lamb
½ yellow onion, grated, juices squeezed out
½ cup chopped pitted prunes
½ cup dried bread crumbs
½ cup crumbled feta cheese
¼ cup dried barberries, soaked for 20 minutes and patted dry
1 tablespoon dried mint
1 tablespoon dried chives
1 egg
½ teaspoon ground turmeric
½ teaspoon ground cinnamon
½ teaspoon garlic powder
Salt and pepper to taste

- In a food processor, pulse together the flour, salt and butter until the mixture turns crumbly. With the food processor still on, gradually pour in the water until the mixture turns into dough that holds together (this will only take about 30 seconds). You may or may not need to use all of the water to achieve this. Remove dough from the food processor and wrap it in plastic wrap. Refrigerate for 1 hour.

- In the meantime, combine all of the ingredients for the filling and knead until well-combined. Refrigerate until ready to use.
- Preheat the oven to 425°F.
- To prepare the pastries, roll the chilled dough out to a ⅛-inch thick rectangle on a lightly floured, flat work surface. Cut the dough into 4 equal portions. Place ¼ of the meat mixture onto the center of each piece of dough. Brush egg wash on the edges of each piece of dough. Fold the dough over the filling, creating a rectangular pocket shape. Press the edges together to seal the pastry (you may use a fork for a decorative effect). Brush the tops of the pastries with egg wash, and use a knife to make two small slits on the top of each one to allow steam to escape. Place the pastries on a greased or parchment paper-lined baking sheet and bake them for about 40 minutes until they are golden brown and the filling has cooked.

Zesty Corn in Lime and Butter

Corn has long been a popular street food in Tehran. Grilled corn on the cob (*balal*) is particularly well-loved. When I was in Tehran I bought a cup of hot corn from a vendor outside a shopping mall and fell in love with it. It was simple yet so flavorful. This recipe is my attempt to recreate it. To add a nice smoky flavor, you can use kernels from freshly grilled corn on the cob.

4 servings

4 tablespoons (½ a stick) unsalted butter
4 cups cooked corn kernels
¼ cup freshly squeezed lime juice
2 teaspoons black pepper
1 teaspoon salt
½ teaspoon ground sumac (optional)
¼ cup chopped cilantro

- Melt the butter in a large saucepan over medium heat.
- Add the rest of the ingredients (minus cilantro) and cook, stirring, until hot. Garnish with cilantro and serve.

Sautéed Kale and White Beans with Fenugreek

Fenugreek adds a unique and complementary flavor to the kale's bitterness and the mild creaminess of the beans.

4 servings

1 tablespoon olive oil
1 small yellow onion, diced
2 garlic cloves, minced
5 cups chopped kale leaves
½ teaspoon ground fenugreek seed
1 (16-ounce) can navy or cannellini beans, drained and rinsed
Salt and pepper to taste

- Heat olive oil in a pan over medium heat. Add onion and garlic and sauté until onion is translucent.
- Add kale leaves and sauté until they have wilted.
- Add fenugreek, beans, salt and pepper and continue to cook, stirring occasionally, for another 3-4 minutes. Serve as a side or mix with a grain like quinoa for a main dish.

Barberry and Dill Cornbread Muffins

Sweet, salty and crumbly, cornbread is a delicious treat. Studded with green dill and red barberries, this recipe would make a festive addition to a holiday meal.

6-8 servings

2 cups yellow cornmeal
1 ½ cups all-purpose flour
2 tablespoons granulated sugar
3 teaspoons baking powder
1 teaspoon baking soda
½ teaspoon salt
4 large eggs
3 cups buttermilk
1 ½ sticks (12 tablespoons) unsalted butter, melted
½ cup finely chopped dill
¼ cup dried barberries, rinsed and patted dry

- Preheat the oven to 425°F.
- In a large bowl, mix together all of the dry ingredients. With your hands, dig a shallow well in the center.
- In a separate bowl, crack open and whisk the eggs. Add the buttermilk and melted butter and whisk well to combine.
- Pour the wet ingredients, along with the dill and barberries, into the center of the dry ingredients. With a spatula, fold the mixture until it is all moistened (there will still be lumps).
- Pour the batter into lightly greased muffin pans. Bake for 20-25 minutes until a fork inserted into the middle of the cornbread comes out clean.

Pomegranate Salsa

The juicy bursts of pomegranate make this zesty salsa so flavorful and delicious. If you love chips and salsa like I do, this is a recipe you'll want to keep on hand.

4-6 servings

2 ripe pomegranates
2 jalapeños, seeds removed, minced
1 bell pepper, seeds removed, diced
1 red onion, diced
1 garlic clove, minced
½ cup chopped cilantro leaves
1 tablespoon olive oil
Juice and zest of 1 lime
½ teaspoon *golpar* powder
Salt and pepper to taste

- Remove the arils (seeds) of the pomegranates and place them in a large bowl. Add the rest of the ingredients and stir well. Serve with tortilla chips.

Pickles

~*~*~

Torshi (which translates as 'sourness') has been made in Iran for centuries, and there are dozens of varieties depending on regional customs. They all consist of various vegetables and fruits pickled in vinegar and salt with herbs and spices.

Pickles are a popular accompaniment to meals, especially rich and heavy ones. Aside from adding flavor, they are also believed to be good for digestion.

Whether you make your own or buy premade torshi from a Persian grocery store, you can serve torshi alongside your meals in small, non-reactive bowls. Try them where you'd normally have traditional cucumber pickles—on a hamburger, for example.

Mixed Vegetable Pickle (Torshi Makhloot)

Pickled Onions (Torshi Piaz)

Pickled Eggplant (Torshi Bademjan)

Pickled Garlic (Seer Torshi)

Mixed Vegetable Pickle (*Torshi Makhloot*)

Prepping all the ingredients for this colorful pickle might seem like a lot of work, but it's totally worth it. Find a helping friend and make a fun afternoon out of it. You can easily double or triple the recipe and give the extra pickles as gifts. Make sure that all of the vegetables and herbs have been washed and completely dried before using. White vinegar will produce a very strong, sour pickle; if you prefer, you can use cider vinegar for a slightly milder taste.

Makes about 6 cups

4 cups white vinegar, plus more as needed
4 tablespoons salt, plus more as needed
1 cauliflower head, finely chopped
6 garlic cloves, minced
3 red onions, diced
3 carrots, shredded or finely chopped
3 celery stalks, finely diced
2 turnips, peeled and diced
2 cups shredded cabbage
1 jalapeño, sliced
½ cup chopped dill
½ cup chopped parsley
½ cup chopped tarragon
½ cup chopped mint
2 tablespoons nigella seeds
2 tablespoons coriander seeds
2 tablespoons dried lime powder
1 tablespoon *golpar* powder
1 tablespoon ground turmeric

- In a saucepan over medium-high heat, bring the vinegar to a simmer. Add the salt and simmer until it has dissolved. Turn off the heat.
- In a large mixing bowl, combine all of the vegetables, herbs and spices. Spoon this mixture into clean, sterilized glass jars

with clean lids (you will probably need 2-3 jars depending on their size). Pour the vinegar mixture over the vegetables in each jar, making sure the jars are filled to the rim and the liquid covers all of the solid ingredients (if not, add more vinegar as needed). Sprinkle an extra teaspoon of salt at the top of each jar.
- Screw the lids on tightly. Store the jars in a cool, dry place for 2 weeks before opening. Refrigerate after opening. The *torshi* will keep for 6 weeks in the refrigerator.

Pickled Onions (*Torshi Piaz*)

I love how this pickle brings out the sweetness in the onions. Onions have long been eaten alongside Persian food and are believed to have antibacterial properties that aid overall health.

Makes about 4 cups

4 cups apple cider vinegar, plus more as needed
4 tablespoons salt, plus more as needed
6 red onions, thinly sliced
½ cup chopped tarragon
½ cup chopped mint
2 tablespoons nigella seeds
2 tablespoons coriander seeds
1 tablespoon *golpar* powder

- In a saucepan over medium-high heat, bring the vinegar to a simmer. Add the salt and simmer until it has dissolved. Turn off the heat.
- Mix the rest of the ingredients together in a large mixing bowl. Spoon the mixture into clean, sterilized glass jars with clean lids.
- Pour the vinegar mixture over the mixture in each jar, making sure the jars are filled to the rim and the liquid covers all of the solid ingredients (if not, add more vinegar as needed). Sprinkle an extra teaspoon of salt at the top of each jar.
- Screw the lids on tightly. Store the jars in a cool, dry place for 2 weeks before opening. Refrigerate after opening. The *torshi* will keep for 6 weeks in the refrigerator.

Pickled Eggplant (*Torshi Bademjan*)

This recipe uses baby eggplants (also known as Indian eggplants), which are just a few inches long, but if you can't find these, you can also make *torshi* out of larger eggplants that have been chopped up.

Makes about 4 cups

4 cups white vinegar, plus more as needed
4 tablespoons salt, plus more as needed
1 teaspoon *golpar* powder
1 teaspoon nigella seeds
1 teaspoon coriander seeds
6 baby eggplants
6 garlic cloves, minced
½ cup chopped mint
½ cup chopped parsley
½ cup chopped tarragon
2-4 small dried red hot peppers

- In a saucepan over medium-high heat, bring the vinegar to a simmer. Add the salt and simmer until it has dissolved. Add the *golpar* powder, nigella and coriander seeds and stir. Turn off the heat.
- Preheat the oven to 350°F. Prick the eggplants in several places with a fork. Place them on a baking sheet and bake them for 40 minutes until softened. Remove them from the oven and let them cool to room temperature. Once the eggplants have cooled, use a knife to make a deep slit in the side of each one—but don't cut them all the way through.
- In a mixing bowl, combine the garlic and herbs. Stuff each eggplant with some of this mixture.
- Pack the eggplants into clean, sterilized glass jars with clean lids. Add a few hot peppers to each jar. Pour the vinegar mixture over the contents of each jar, making sure the jar is full to the rim. If needed, add more vinegar to the top. Sprinkle an extra teaspoon of salt over the top of each jar.

- Screw the lids on tightly. Store the jars in a cool, dry place for 2 weeks before opening. Refrigerate after opening. The *torshi* will keep for 6 weeks in the refrigerator.

Pickled Garlic (*Seer Torshi*)

This recipe reminds me of my dad, who makes pickled garlic in huge jars that have been in the pantry at my parents' house for years. You can use any type of vinegar, but I like the combination of the garlic and balsamic vinegar as the vinegar really enhances the sweetness of the garlic over time.

Makes about 4 cups

10 heads of garlic
4 cups balsamic vinegar, plus more as needed
4 tablespoons salt, plus more as needed
3 teaspoons honey

- Break the garlic heads apart into cloves. Remove the outer skins of the cloves, leaving the thinner inner skins intact. Pack the cloves into clean, sterilized glass jars with clean lids.
- In a separate bowl, mix together the vinegar, salt and honey. Pour this liquid over the garlic cloves, covering them completely and filling the jars to the rim. If needed, add more vinegar. Sprinkle the top of each jar with an extra teaspoon of salt. Cover the tops of the jars with plastic wrap and screw the lids on tight.
- Store in a cool, dry, dark place for at least 1 year. Check the jars every once in a while to see if you need to add more vinegar and salt or open the jars to release built up gas. Iranians say that 7-year garlic *torshi* is at its best—if you can avoid eating it for that long!

Desserts

~*~*~

Desserts are the jewels of a Persian meal. Popular Persian desserts include fruit, ice cream, baklava, pastries, cookies, nougats and cakes. French-style pastries, such as éclairs and cream puffs, are very popular. Notes of saffron and rosewater elevate ordinary sweets to another level.

In Iran, pastries are classified into two categories: shirini tar (wet pastry) and shirini khoshk (dry pastry). Dry pastries include cookies, biscuits and sweet breads. Wet pastries include those with cream or filling.

Fruit Leather (Lavashak)

Baklava (Baqlava)

Rice Flour Cardamom Cookies (Nan Berenji)

Quick and Easy Saffron-Rose Ice Cream (Bastani)

Frozen Rice Noodles with Rosewater and Lime (Faloodeh)

Saffron Rice Pudding (Shole Zard)

Milky Rice Pudding (Shir Berenj)

Honey-Almond Brittle (Sohan Asal)

Spiced Carrot Ice Cream Float (Havij Bastani)

Date and Chocolate Chip Cake Roll

Sour Cherry Sundae

Persimmon Cheesecake with a Chocolate Crust

Fresh Fig and Peach Tart

Orange Clove Almond Cookies

Fruit Leather (*Lavashak*)

Fruit leather is hugely popular in Iran. As a kid I was always excited when a visiting relative would bring us some *lavashak,* and I could peel it off of its plastic packaging and enjoy its mouthwatering sour flavor. Making *lavashak* at home is incredibly easy. You don't need any fancy equipment, either—just an oven (or the sun), a baking sheet and some parchment paper.

4-6 servings

4 pounds of your favorite stone fruits (peaches, nectarines, plums, cherries, apricots)
½ cup water
1 tablespoon freshly squeezed lemon juice

- Wash the fruits, cut them in half and remove all of their pits.
- Combine the fruit, water and lemon juice in a large pot and cook over low heat until the fruits are completely softened (about 30-40 minutes). Stir occasionally to prevent the fruit from sticking to the pot.
- Remove the fruit from the stove and puree it in a blender or food processor.
- Preheat oven to 175°F.
- Line a large baking sheet with parchment paper and spread the puree across it in a thin layer. Bake for 6 hours or until the puree is no longer sticky. (Alternatively, if you live in a sunny climate, cover the puree with cheesecloth and let it sit outside in direct sunlight for 4 days.) Let it cool, and then slice it into strips with a pizza cutter. Enjoy!

Baklava (*Baqlava*)

Baklava truly must be one of the most indulgent desserts on the planet. Who can resist the crisp, flaky, buttery sheets of phyllo dough dripping with sugary syrup? Baklava is consumed across much of the Middle East and Europe. The Persian version uses cardamom, rosewater and saffron to add a distinctly Persian flavor to the classic dessert.

10-12 servings

2 cups slivered almonds
2 cups shelled unsalted pistachios (or you can use hazelnuts)
1 teaspoon ground cardamom
Pinch of salt
1 cup plus 2 tablespoons granulated sugar
1 cup water
⅛ teaspoon powdered saffron
½ cup rosewater
1 package frozen phyllo dough, thawed (20 total sheets)
1 cup unsalted butter, melted
2 tablespoons honey

Filling:

- Place a pan on the stove and turn the heat on to medium. Add the nuts to the pan and toast, stirring, until fragrant. Remove the nuts from the pan and grind them in a food processor until crumbly.
- In a mixing bowl, combine the ground nuts, 2 tablespoons of sugar, a pinch of salt, and the cardamom and mix well.

Syrup:

- In a small saucepan over medium heat, bring 1 cup of water and 1 cup of sugar to a boil, stirring occasionally, until the sugar is completely dissolved.
- Reduce heat to low. Add saffron and rosewater and simmer for another 5 minutes. Remove from heat and set aside to cool.

To assemble:

- Preheat oven to 350°F.
- Line a baking sheet with parchment paper. Using a pastry brush, butter the surface of the parchment paper with some melted butter.
- Place 1 sheet of phyllo dough on the baking sheet and brush with melted butter. Repeat 4 more times until 5 sheets are stacked.
- Spread a third of the nut mixture across the entire surface of the dough in an even layer.
- Stack 5 more sheets of phyllo dough over the nuts, brushing each one with melted butter before adding the next.
- Spread another third of the nut mixture across the top of the dough.
- Add 5 more sheets of buttered phyllo dough.
- Spread the remaining third of the nut mixture across the top.
- Top the baklava with the remaining 5 sheets of phyllo dough, buttering each.
- Use a sharp knife to cut the baklava into diamond shapes about 2 inches long. Bake on the center rack of the oven for 30 minutes or until the top is golden brown. Then remove the tray from the oven and pour half of the syrup over the baklava. Place the tray back in the oven and bake for another 5-7 minutes.
- Remove tray from the oven and pour the remaining syrup over the baklava. Then drizzle the honey over the top. Let the baklava cool before serving. For best results, serve the next day. You can store the baklava in an airtight container for up to 1 week.

Rice Flour Cardamom Cookies (*Nan Berenji*)

This is an easy to make gluten-free cookie that is light and delicately flavored. It goes perfectly with a cup of tea. You can adjust this basic recipe to flavor the cookies differently; for example, you could use cinnamon or citrus zest.

Makes approximately 20 cookies

⅓ cup canola oil
⅔ cup confectioner's sugar
2 eggs
2 ¼ cups rice flour
¼ teaspoon baking powder
1 teaspoon ground cardamom
Poppy seeds, for garnish

- In a large bowl, combine the canola oil and sugar.
- Crack the eggs into a separate bowl and whisk together. Add the eggs to the oil and sugar. Add the flour, baking powder and cardamom and mix until a thick dough forms. Cover and refrigerate for 30 minutes.
- Preheat oven to 350°F. Lightly grease a baking sheet or line it with parchment paper. Take a golf ball-sized amount of the dough and roll it between your palms to form a ball. Flatten it slightly and place on the baking sheet. Repeat with the remaining dough. Sprinkle the top of each cookie with poppy seeds.
- Bake cookies until they become firm and crack on top, about 15-20 minutes. The cookies will be white but should have turned slightly golden on the bottom. Remove them from the oven and set aside to cool completely before removing them from the pan. Eat immediately or store in an airtight container for up to 1 week.

Quick and Easy Saffron-Rose Ice Cream (*Bastani*)

Traditional Persian saffron ice cream is rich and decadent, yellow and white with chunks of frozen cream. You can easily find it in Persian grocery stores. For this recipe I wanted to create a quick version that you can make yourself using store-bought vanilla ice cream. While the authentic version of the ice cream doesn't have vanilla, the flavors of the rosewater and saffron mask most of the vanilla taste.

2-4 servings

1 cup heavy whipping cream
1 pint vanilla ice cream, softened
Pinch of saffron threads
3 tablespoons rosewater
¼ cup chopped unsalted pistachios

- Pour the whipping cream into a shallow dish, like a pie pan or baking sheet, and place it in the freezer. Freeze for a few hours until the cream turns solid. Remove from the freezer and break up the cream into small chunks using a fork.
- Use a mortar and pestle, or a spice grinder, to grind the saffron threads into a powder. Combine saffron powder with the rosewater and stir well.
- Add the saffron and rosewater, pistachios, and chunks of cream to the softened ice cream and stir well to combine. The ice cream should turn yellow from the saffron.
- When the ingredients are well-combined, pour the mixture into a frozen container and refreeze until solid. Serve plain or sandwiched between wafer cookies.

Frozen Rice Noodles with Rosewater and Lime (*Faloodeh*)

These cold, crisp, sweet noodles are usually eaten alone or alongside ice cream.

4 servings

1 cup water, plus more as needed
1 cup granulated sugar
1 tablespoon rosewater
2 ounces very thin rice noodles
Lemon or lime wedges

- In a small saucepan, combine sugar and 1 cup of water and bring to a boil. Once the sugar has dissolved, add the rosewater and stir. Remove from heat and let the syrup cool.
- Bring a kettle of water to a boil. Break the rice noodles up into 1-2 inch lengths. Place them in a heatproof bowl or pot and pour in enough boiling water to cover them. Allow the noodles to cook this way until they have just softened, about 5 minutes. Drain the noodles and rinse them in cold water to stop the cooking process.
- In a freezer-proof dish, add the noodles and pour the syrup over them.
- Place the dish in the freezer and freeze for 1 hour. Remove from the freezer and use a fork to stir the mixture, breaking it up a little bit. Place it back in the freezer and freeze for another 2 hours.
- To serve, scrape out some of the frozen noodles into bowls and squeeze generous amounts of lemon or lime juice over them.

Saffron Rice Pudding (*Shole Zard*)

This exquisite pudding is fragrant with saffron, rosewater, and cinnamon, with a pleasing crunch from the nuts. It can be served either warm or cold.

6-8 servings

2 cups basmati rice
2 cups granulated sugar
2 tablespoons saffron water
½ cup slivered almonds
¼ cup ground, unsalted pistachios
⅓ cup rosewater
2 tablespoons unsalted butter, melted
Water

Garnish:
2 tablespoons slivered almonds
2 tablespoons chopped unsalted pistachios
1-2 tablespoons ground cinnamon

- Soak the rice in water overnight. When you're ready to use it, drain and rinse the rice and place it into a large, heavy-bottomed pot.
- Add 12 cups of water to the pot and bring it to a gentle boil over medium heat.
- Reduce the heat to low and cook, stirring occasionally, for 40 minutes or until the rice is soft.
- Add the sugar and stir until the sugar has dissolved.
- Add saffron water, almonds, pistachios and butter. Stir well until saffron water is well-incorporated throughout. Simmer for 15 minutes over low heat.
- Add the rosewater, then cover and cook for another 15 minutes.
- To serve, pour the pudding into a large serving bowl. Garnish with ground cinnamon, almonds and pistachios.

Milky Rice Pudding (*Shir Berenj*)

Relax with a bowl of this warm, sweet and comforting dessert.

4-6 servings

1 cup basmati rice
1 cup water
3 cups whole milk
¼ cup granulated sugar
⅓ cup rosewater
½ teaspoon ground cardamom

Toppings:
Honey
Ground cinnamon
Raisins (optional)

- Soak rice in water overnight. Drain and rinse before using.
- In a large, heavy-bottomed pot, add rice and 1 cup of water. Bring to a gentle boil over medium-low heat, and then reduce heat to low and cook until the water is absorbed.
- Add milk to the rice 1 cup at a time, stirring constantly.
- Cook for 30-40 minutes over low heat until the milk has been absorbed by the rice.
- Add sugar and rosewater and stir well.
- Cook for another 15-20 minutes on low. When the sugar has dissolved and the pudding is thick, remove from heat and let it cool.
- Serve warm, topped with honey, cinnamon and raisins.

Honey-Almond Brittle (*Sohan Asal*)

These tasty treats have a nice, deep, caramel-like flavor. Serve them with tea.

4-8 servings

1 cup granulated sugar
3 tablespoons honey
4 tablespoons canola, corn or vegetable oil
2 tablespoons rosewater
1 cup slivered almonds, plus more for garnish
¼ teaspoon ground saffron threads
Pinch of ground cardamom

- Cover a large baking sheet with parchment paper.
- In a medium saucepan, combine the sugar, honey, oil and rosewater. Cook over medium heat, stirring constantly with a wooden spoon, for about 5-7 minutes or until sugar is completely dissolved.
- Lower the heat and add 1 cup of slivered almonds. Cook for another 5-7 minutes, stirring constantly, until the mixture is golden brown and foamy.
- Add saffron and stir well. Remove from heat and drop spoonfuls of the mixture onto the parchment paper. Sprinkle more slivered almonds on top of each spoonful.
- Let the *sohan* cool completely before removing them from the parchment paper. Store them in an airtight container and wait a day before eating.

Spiced Carrot Ice Cream Float (*Havij Bastani*)

This is a unique Persian treat combining fresh, sweet carrot juice with saffron ice cream. You may not have considered putting carrot juice in a dessert, but it's a trick that works surprisingly well. If you enjoy desserts made with pumpkin, you'll probably like this. Enjoy this ice cream float on a hot day, and get a little extra vitamin A too!

4 servings

8 scoops saffron ice cream (store-bought or homemade; for the latter, see recipe on page 214)
4 cups pure carrot juice
½ teaspoon ground cinnamon
½ teaspoon ground cardamom
½ teaspoon ground ginger
⅛ teaspoon ground nutmeg
¼ cup chopped pistachios

- Set out 4 glasses. Fill each with 2 scoops of ice cream and 1 cup of carrot juice.
- Mix the spices together in a small bowl. Sprinkle a pinch of this spice mixture on top of each float. Top each float with a spoonful of chopped pistachios and serve immediately.

Date and Chocolate Chip Cake Roll

Light, airy cake rolls (known as *rolette*) are a popular dessert, especially those delicately flavored with saffron and rosewater. Here is a richer version combining dates and chocolate chips.

6-8 servings

Cake:
4 eggs
1 cup granulated sugar
1 teaspoon vanilla extract
1 cup flour
1 teaspoon baking powder
¼ cup rosewater

Filling:
1 cup pitted dates, chopped
½ cup granulated sugar
½ cup water
2 cups heavy whipping cream
1 cup confectioner's sugar
½ cup semi-sweet chocolate chips

Garnish:
Whipped cream
Chocolate chips and/or melted chocolate
Rose petals

Cake:

- Preheat oven to 350°F. Line a large baking sheet with parchment paper and set it aside.
- In a stand mixer, or a large bowl with an electric mixer, beat the eggs until they are fluffy (about 1 minute).
- Add sugar and vanilla and mix well (about 2-3 minutes).
- Gently fold in the flour and baking powder using a spatula until the batter is smooth.

- Spread the batter onto the parchment-lined baking sheet and bake for 15 minutes.

Filling:

- In a small saucepan over low heat, add dates, sugar and water. Bring to a boil. Cook for about 15 minutes, stirring occasionally, until the mixture becomes smooth and thick. Remove from heat and set aside.
- Using an electric or stand mixer, beat the whipping cream until peaks form.
- Add the sugar, chocolate chips, and date mixture to the cream and stir well to combine.

To assemble:

- Lift the parchment paper and cake off from the baking sheet and gently peel the paper from the cake. Place the cake on a flat, smooth surface.
- Using a pastry brush, brush the top of the cake with rosewater.
- With a spatula, spread the date filling evenly over the cake.
- Starting from one of its short sides, gently roll the cake up with the filling on the inside.
- Place the cake on a serving platter with the seam side down.
- Garnish the cake with dollops of whipped cream, a drizzle of chocolate and/or a sprinkle of chocolate chips, and rose petals.

Sour Cherry Sundae

In Iran, I once tried a vanilla ice cream bar that was covered in a sour cherry coating. It was one of the best ice cream treats I've ever had in my life. The combination of the sweet vanilla and the tart, fruity cherries is divine. This simple recipe mimics the flavors of that amazing ice cream bar.

2-4 servings

1 pint good quality vanilla ice cream
1 cup sour cherry preserves

- Scoop ice cream into bowls. Top with preserves. Enjoy!

Persimmon Cheesecake with a Chocolate Crust

I love persimmons. There's something about their intense, floral sweetness and slightly syrupy quality that make me feel like I'm eating something rather luxurious. Naturally, I thought to pair them with another decadent indulgence—cheesecake. The slight tanginess of the cheesecake balances out the sweetness of the persimmon. Choose very soft, ripe Hachiya persimmons, which are better for cooking than their firmer Fuyu cousins.

8-10 servings

Crust:
2 cups chocolate cookie crumbs
¼ cup unsalted butter, melted

Filling:
4 (8-ounce) packages cream cheese, softened
1 very ripe Hachiya persimmon, pureed in a blender
⅔ cup honey
1 teaspoon vanilla extract
4 eggs
Zest of 1 lemon

Topping:
2 ripe Hachiya or Fuyu persimmons, sliced into ¼-inch rounds

- Preheat oven to 325°F.

- Mix together the cookie crumbs and butter. Press the mixture onto the bottom (and slightly up the sides) of a 9-inch springform pan.

- With an electric mixer, beat the cream cheese, persimmon puree, honey and vanilla extract until smooth. Turn the mixer speed to low and add the eggs, one at a time, waiting until each one is just blended before adding the next.

- Spread the filling over the crust. Place the cheesecake in the oven and bake for 55 minutes, or until the center is set.

- Remove cake from the oven and let it cool before removing the pan rim. Arrange persimmon slices across the top of the cake. Refrigerate for at least 6 hours before serving.

Fresh Fig and Peach Tart

This beautiful tart is very simple to make—the only part that needs baking is the crust.

4-8 servings

1 package pre-made pastry dough
8 ounces mascarpone cheese
2 tablespoons honey or confectioner's sugar
1 tablespoon lemon zest
1 teaspoon vanilla extract
Pinch of salt
2 Black Mission figs, sliced
2 ripe peaches, sliced

Garnish:
Honey
Whipped cream
Dried rose petals

- Preheat oven to 400°F.
- Line a 10-inch tart pan with pastry dough. Trim off any excess. Place a sheet of aluminum foil over the dough and pour dry beans or rice into the pan to weigh down the foil. Place the pan in the oven and bake the dough for 15 minutes. Remove the foil and beans/rice and bake for another 5-10 minutes, until the tart crust turns golden brown. Remove from the oven and set aside.
- In a large mixing bowl, combine mascarpone, honey, lemon zest, vanilla and salt and stir well to combine.
- Spread the filling onto the tart crust. Arrange fig and peach slices across the top of the tart. Drizzle the tart with honey, add dollops of whipped cream, and sprinkle with rose petals.

Orange Clove Almond Cookies

These simple confections made with ground almonds are very popular in Iran. Similar to marzipan, they can be molded into various shapes and tinted with food coloring. You can make different variations on these by adding whatever flavorings you like. For this recipe, I decided to use a sweet, spicy blend of oranges and cloves.

4-6 servings

¾ cup finely ground almonds
¾ cup confectioner's sugar, plus more for coating
⅛ teaspoon ground cloves
5 tablespoons orange blossom water
Zest of ½ an orange
Whole cloves, for garnish

- In a bowl, mix all ingredients and knead well until they form a thick paste. Press the paste into a baking pan lined with parchment paper. Let it sit for 30 minutes.
- Remove the paste from the pan and place it on a flat surface. Peel off the parchment paper. Using a pizza cutter, slice the paste diagonally into bite-sized diamonds.
- Roll each of the diamonds in confectioner's sugar and stick a whole clove in the center of each.
- Eat immediately or store in the refrigerator in an airtight container for up to one week.

Beverages

~*~*~

Persian-Style Tea

Pomegranate Spritzer (Sharbat-e Anar)

Sour Cherry Spritzer (Sharbat-e Albaloo)

Rose Lemonade (Sharbat-e Ab Limoo)

Honeydew and Mint Smoothie

Cantaloupe and Rose Smoothie

Banana Smoothie (Shir Moz)

Yogurt Soda with Mint (Doogh)

Tea

You may know *chai* as a spiced black tea containing cinnamon, cloves and other spices. This version is actually known as *masala chai* and originated in South Asia. *Chai,* however, is simply the word for tea in Farsi and Hindi.

Tea is undoubtedly the most important beverage in Persian culture. Iranians drink tea in the morning, afternoon and evening. It is normally served hot, not iced—even in the middle of summer. Black teas are the most popular and are sometimes flavored with additions such as cinnamon or rosewater. Herbal teas, such as chamomile and borage flower, are also consumed, especially for their medicinal purposes.

It is customary to offer guests tea after they arrive. At a dinner party, tea is usually offered both before and after dinner. Most Iranians serve tea in glass teacups with something sweet offered on the side (usually sugar cubes, honey, dried fruit, and/or pastries). Visiting a teahouse is a traditional pastime in Iran that lives on today.

Persian-Style Tea

There's nothing like a simple cup of tea to evoke togetherness, conversation and relaxation.

8-12 servings

4 tablespoons loose black tea leaves
Water

Optional flavorings (per pot of tea):
Cardamom pods, pierced (2-3 pods)
Cinnamon sticks (1 or 2)
Dried apples (3-4 slices)
Jasmine flowers (1 tablespoon dried)

- Fill a kettle with water and bring it to a boil on the stove.
- Place tea leaves inside a teapot, fill it with boiling water and put on the lid. Add a flavoring agent if desired.
- Refill the kettle with water and bring it to a boil again. Remove the kettle lid and set the teapot on top of the kettle. Reduce heat to low and let the tea simmer for at least 10 minutes. You're basically creating a concentrated tea that will be diluted with boiling water from the kettle (the kettle also keeps the concentrated tea warm).
- To serve, pour tea from the teapot into glass teacups, adjusting its strength with boiling water from the kettle as necessary. Serve with sugar cubes, dried fruits such as raisins or dates, pastries, or other sweets if desired.

Pomegranate Spritzer (*Sharbat-e Anar*)

This is a delicious and refreshing drink to serve on a hot day. I like to enhance the pomegranate flavor with the addition of lime juice and orange blossom water.

4-6 servings

1 cup water
1 cup granulated sugar
1 liter club soda, seltzer or sparkling water
¾ cup pomegranate syrup
2 tablespoons freshly squeezed lime juice
1 tablespoon orange blossom water
Ice cubes

- In a small saucepan, combine the water and sugar. Bring to a boil, stirring, until sugar has dissolved. Remove from heat and let cool.
- When the syrup has cooled, add it to a pitcher with the soda, pomegranate syrup, lime juice and orange blossom water and stir well. Pour into glasses over ice cubes and serve immediately.

Sour Cherry Spritzer (*Sharbat-e Albaloo*)

Sour cherry syrup mixed with water and ice is a classic summer drink in Iran. I like to make a sparkling version for a little extra fun and refreshment.

4-6 servings

1 cup granulated sugar
1 cup water
2 cups sour cherry juice
1 liter club soda, seltzer or sparkling water
Ice cubes

- In a saucepan, add the sugar and water and bring to a boil. Add the cherry juice and boil, stirring, until the sugar has dissolved and the mixture thickens and becomes syrupy. Remove from heat and let cool.
- In a pitcher, combine the cherry syrup and soda and stir well. Pour into glasses over ice cubes and serve immediately.

Rose Lemonade (*Sharbat-e Ab Limoo*)

Classic lemonade gets an exotic twist with the addition of rosewater in this simple recipe.

4-6 servings

3 cups water, plus more as needed
1 cup granulated sugar
1 cup freshly squeezed lemon juice
¼ cup rosewater
Ice cubes

- In a small saucepan, bring the sugar and 3 cups of water to a boil, stirring, until the sugar has dissolved. Remove from heat and let cool.
- In a pitcher, combine the syrup, lemon juice, rosewater, and enough water to fill the rest of the pitcher. Stir well. Pour into glasses over ice cubes and serve immediately.

Honeydew and Mint Smoothie

The combination of sweet honeydew with fresh mint produces a fresh, flavorful, and wonderfully cooling drink.

3-4 servings

Flesh of ½ a honeydew melon, cubed
2 cups ice
1 cup water
1 tablespoon freshly squeezed lime juice
2 tablespoons granulated sugar
1 handful mint leaves, chopped, plus a few whole ones for garnish

- In a blender, puree all ingredients until smooth. Pour into glasses and garnish with mint leaves. Serve immediately.

Cantaloupe and Rose Smoothie

In this recipe, rosewater enhances cantaloupe's naturally sweet and floral flavor.

4-6 servings

Flesh of ½ a cantaloupe, cubed
2 cups ice
1 cup water
2 tablespoons rosewater
1 tablespoon freshly squeezed lemon juice
½ teaspoon ground cardamom
Dried crushed rose petals (for garnish)

- In a blender, puree all ingredients until smooth. Pour into glasses and garnish with dried rose petals. Serve immediately.

Banana Smoothie (*Shir Moz*)

This is a super simple recipe that is traditionally prepared as a snack for children. It's an easy way to use up any ripe bananas you might have lying around. I particularly enjoy it with vanilla-flavored almond milk in place of regular cow's milk.

2 servings

2 ripe bananas
1 ½ cups milk (may substitute a non-dairy milk if desired)
8 ice cubes

- In a blender, puree all ingredients until smooth. Pour into glasses and serve immediately.

Yogurt Soda with Mint (*Doogh*)

Doogh makes a tasty and refreshing accompaniment to many Persian meals, especially kabobs. In its simplest form, *doogh* is watered down yogurt, served cold—but most people add salt and/or mint leaves. It can be made with still or sparkling water, but I prefer sparkling. I find it difficult to explain the appeal of *doogh* to my American friends, since we're not used to salty beverages here in the U.S.—it's one of those things that you just have to try!

4 servings

1 liter club soda, seltzer or sparkling water
2 cups yogurt
1 teaspoon salt (or more to taste)
¼ cup chopped mint leaves (or 1 tablespoon dried mint leaves)
Ice cubes

- Mix all ingredients together in a pitcher until the *doogh* is smooth and there are no lumps of yogurt remaining. Pour into glasses and serve immediately.

Index

"

"Sweet" Rice with Barberries, Nuts, Carrots and Candied Orange Peel, 159, 165

A

A Traditional Breakfast Spread, 54, 55
aash, 39, 82, 90
Aash Reshteh, 81, 82
Aash-e Maast, 81
Abdoogh Khiar, 81, 86
Abgoosht, 81, 87
accompaniments, 15
Adaas Polow, 159, 170
Adaasi, 81, 85
Advieh, 35
ajil, 22
Albaloo Polow, 159, 167
almonds, 22, 47, 62, 73, 106, 119, 165, 180, 211, 216, 218, 226
Almonds, 22
appetizers, 15, 49
apple, 30, 77, 118, 173, 178, 205
Apple, Raisin and Garlic Rice, 159, 178
apples, 25, 27, 118, 178, 229
apricots, 11, 106, 118, 141, 210
arils, 24, 46, 201, *See* Pomegranate
artichoke, 73, 95
Artichoke and Herb Soup, 81, 95
Artichoke Couscous Salad with Dill Yogurt Dressing, 69, 73
arugula, 78
asparagus, 105
Asparagus, 97, 105

B

Baghali Polow, 159, 168
baguette, 68, 152, 153
baking powder, 63, 98, 99, 101, 102, 104, 105, 106, 107, 200, 213, 220
baking soda, 200

Baklava, 209, 211
Banana Smoothie, 227, 235
bananas, 59, 235
barbari, 20, 183
barberries, 27, 30, 75, 98, 141, 165, 166, 196, 200
barberry, 13, 166
Barberry, 27, 182, 200
Barberry and Dill Cornbread, 182, 200
Barg, 123, 124, 129, 182, 190
barley, 11, 21, 84
Barley, 21, 81, 84
basil, 13, 31, 72, 78, 80, 86, 131
Basil, 183
basmati, 5, 19, 141, 143, 160, 164, 175, 180, 190, 216, 217
Bastani, 209, 214, 219
bay leaves, 84
beans, 13, 17, 23, 24, 31, 35, 42, 45, 52, 80, 82, 83, 87, 108, 109, 113, 114, 156, 168, 171, 177, 189, 199, 225
Beans, 23, 45, 81, 82, 139, 159, 168, 182, 189, 199
Beef, 17, 108, 110, 112, 119, 123, 124, 129, 130, 138, 152, 159, 171, 182, 192
Beef and Kumquat Stew, 108, 119
Beef and Potato Patties, 182, 192
Beef, Eggplant and Tomato Stew, 108, 110
Beef, Potato and Split Pea Stew, 108, 112
bell peppers, 132, 143
berries, 27, 33, 59
Beverages, 7, 227
black pepper, 35, 149, 179, 198
borage, 32, 228
Borage, 32
Borani Bademjan, 182, 187
Borani Esfenaj, 182, 186
braises, 39
Braising, 42
bread, 3, 15, 19, 20, 22, 29, 31, 47, 55, 58, 65, 67, 68, 83, 84, 85, 86, 87, 89, 91, 93, 95, 125, 126, 127, 128, 129, 130, 132,

239

134, 146, 153, 158, 163, 183, 184, 189, 193, 196
breakfast, 17, 19, 21, 31, 55, 59, 67, 104, 159, 189
Breakfast, 7, 54, 55, 61
broccoli, 75, 105
brown basmati, 19
Brown rice, 164
Brown Rice, 164
bulgur wheat, 21, 56
butter, 13, 29, 36, 43, 55, 56, 59, 61, 63, 65, 66, 68, 88, 90, 95, 96, 98, 99, 101, 102, 104, 105, 106, 107, 120, 121, 126, 127, 128, 129, 139, 140, 150, 152, 153, 160, 161, 163, 165, 166, 167, 168, 169, 170, 171, 172, 173, 174, 177, 178, 179, 180, 181, 196, 198, 200, 211, 212, 216, 223
Butter, 55, 68, 98, 99, 101, 102, 104, 105, 106, 107, 182, 183, 198
buttermilk, 200
butternut squash, 92, 179
Butternut Squash Rice, 159, 179

C

cabbage, 135, 136, 143, 173, 174, 203
Cabbage Rice with Lamb Meatballs, 159, 173
canola oil, 36, 62, 65, 67, 78, 82, 85, 88, 90, 92, 94, 99, 101, 102, 110, 112, 113, 115, 117, 118, 119, 130, 143, 147, 149, 150, 156, 160, 163, 173, 175, 177, 181, 190, 192, 193, 195, 213
cantaloupe, 77, 133, 234
Cantaloupe and Rose Smoothie, 227, 234
capers, 74
caramelized onions, 42
Caramelized onions, 28
cardamom, 13, 33, 35, 63, 92, 211, 213, 217, 218, 219, 234
Cardamom, 33, 54, 63, 209, 213, 229
Cardamom-Orange Pancakes with Rose Syrup, 54, 63
carrot, 30, 71, 74, 166, 219
carrots, 30, 40, 75, 84, 85, 94, 96, 165, 166, 180, 203
Carrots, 30, 159, 165
cashews, 121

Caspian Sea, 10, 12, 18, 159
cauliflower, 181, 203
celery, 74, 84, 85, 94, 95, 96, 115, 116, 203
chai, 36, 228
Cheese, 18, 54, 55, 68
cheeses. *See* Cheese
cherries, 11, 26, 167, 210, 222
chicken, 4, 13, 17, 30, 33, 40, 44, 71, 80, 85, 88, 90, 92, 94, 95, 96, 110, 115, 116, 117, 119, 120, 121, 124, 128, 141, 142, 175, 176
Chicken and Celery Stew, 108, 115
Chicken Curry Pot Pie, 108, 121
Chicken in Pomegranate-Walnut Sauce, 108, 117
Chicken, Fennel and Tomato Stew, 108, 120
Chicken, Rice and Yogurt 'Casserole', 159, 175
Chickpea and Peach Salad with Curried Balsamic Vinaigrette, 69, 76
chickpeas, 76, 80, 82, 87, 90
Chickpeas, 24, 69, 80
chili powder, 65, 150
Chilled Yogurt Soup, 81, 86
chives, 13, 31, 98, 99, 113, 145, 190, 195, 196
Chives, 183
Chocolate chips, 220
chocolate cookie crumbs, 223
cilantro, 13, 31, 34, 51, 61, 76, 82, 90, 95, 98, 106, 113, 135, 140, 150, 151, 169, 177, 195, 198, 201
Cilantro, 183
cinnamon, 13, 17, 35, 56, 65, 67, 74, 85, 87, 92, 104, 110, 112, 115, 116, 118, 119, 135, 143, 144, 156, 165, 170, 171, 173, 180, 190, 195, 196, 213, 216, 217, 219, 228
Cinnamon, 54, 56, 229
Citrus fruits, 28
Citrus zester, 40
clarified butter, 36
cloth lid cover, 38
cloves, 35, 73, 82, 84, 85, 87, 88, 90, 92, 94, 95, 96, 102, 110, 115, 118, 119, 120, 121, 129, 139, 140, 141, 143, 145, 147, 152, 153, 156, 171, 178, 181, 186, 187,

190, 193, 194, 195, 199, 203, 206, 208, 226, 228
club soda, 230, 231, 236
coconut oil, 36
Colander, 38
Cooking fats, 35
Coriander, 34
coriander seeds, 203, 205, 206
corn, 135, 154, 198, 218
cornmeal, 200
couscous, 73
cream, 26, 55, 59, 60, 68, 92, 96, 133, 209, 214, 215, 219, 220, 221, 222, 223, 225
Creamy Fried Eggplant Dip, 137, 182, 193
Creamy Potato Salad with Chicken, 69, 71
Creamy Saffron Potato Soup, 81, 96
cucumber, 70, 73, 78, 184, 202
Cucumber, Tomato and Onion Salad, 69, 70, 125, 137, 156
cucumbers, 25, 55, 86, 185
Cucumbers, 25
cumin, 13, 22, 35, 67, 74, 85, 90, 92, 119, 135, 143, 144, 156, 165, 170, 173, 175, 177, 180, 195
curry powder, 76, 121

D

Date and Chocolate Chip Cake Roll, 209, 220
dates, 13, 21, 25, 80, 104, 170, 220, 221, 229
Dates, 25, 69, 80, 104
dessert, 10, 21, 26, 49, 59, 104, 133, 211, 217, 219, 220
Desserts, 7, 209
dietary restrictions, 51
dill, 31, 71, 73, 90, 98, 131, 140, 141, 142, 152, 153, 158, 168, 169, 200, 203
dill pickle, 131, 152
Dill Rice with Favas, 139, 159, 168
dolmeh, 29, 143, 190, 191
Dolmeh Barg-e Mo, 182, 190
Dolmeh Felfel, 138, 143
Doogh, 227, 236
Dried Apricot, 97, 106
dried fruit, 13, 141, 228
dried herbs, 51

Dried limes, 34
Dried rose petals, 34, 63, 92, 225
duck, 17, 117
Dutch oven, 39, 92, 110, 112, 113, 115, 117, 118, 119, 120, 121, 139, 175, 176

E

egg, 27, 58, 63, 65, 66, 97, 141, 150, 175, 196, 197
Egg Entrees, 7, 97
eggplant, 13, 29, 44, 46, 67, 102, 110, 111, 132, 187, 206
Eggplant and Tofu Scramble, 54, 67
eggplants, 5, 29, 102, 110, 143, 145, 146, 193, 206
Eggplants, 29
eggs, 13, 55, 58, 61, 65, 66, 67, 71, 88, 97, 98, 99, 101, 102, 104, 105, 106, 107, 141, 145, 146, 180, 189, 192, 200, 213, 220, 223
Eggs, 54, 55, 58, 65, 97, 138, 145
entrées, 15, 39
equipment, 38, 160, 210
Eshkeneh, 81, 88
Etiquette, 7, 48

F

Faloodeh, 209, 215
Farsi, 9, 28, 30, 35, 51, 58, 149, 228
fava, 24, 168
fava beans, 24, 168
fennel, 65, 120
fennel seeds, 65
fenugreek, 13, 31, 32, 88, 107, 113, 150, 199
Fenugreek, 31, 81, 88, 182, 199
Fesenjan, 108, 117
feta, 18, 55, 61, 67, 72, 73, 137, 156, 158, 196
fig, 55, 225
Fig, Honey and Cream Cheese Toasts, 54
figs, 68, 225
fillet, 17, 129, 150
fish, 5, 12, 18, 33, 37, 40, 44, 140, 150, 151, 169
Fish, 18, 138, 140, 150, 169

241

Fish with Spicy Tamarind Sauce, 138, 150
flank steak, 78
flatbread, 55, 145, 183
flatbreads, 20
flour, 20, 59, 61, 63, 88, 90, 96, 97, 98, 99, 101, 102, 104, 105, 106, 107, 135, 137, 150, 192, 196, 200, 213, 220
Fresh Fig and Peach Tart, 209, 225
Fresh Vegetable and Herb Platter, 182, 183
frittata, 97
Fruit, 6, 13, 54, 55, 59, 69, 77, 123, 133, 209, 210
Fruit Leather, 209, 210
fruits. *See* Fruit
Frying pan, 39

G

garbanzo beans, 82, 87
gard-e limoo, 34
Garden Pasta Salad with Kale and Barberries, 69, 75
garlic, 13, 58, 65, 67, 73, 74, 78, 82, 84, 85, 87, 88, 90, 92, 94, 95, 96, 102, 105, 107, 110, 115, 116, 118, 119, 120, 121, 126, 129, 134, 135, 139, 140, 141, 143, 144, 145, 147, 150, 152, 153, 156, 168, 171, 178, 180, 181, 186, 187, 190, 193, 194, 195, 196, 199, 201, 203, 206, 208
garmi, 14
garnish, 19, 34, 42, 67, 82, 86, 96, 112, 119, 140, 145, 150, 151, 185, 187, 193, 213, 218, 226, 233, 234
Genoa salami, 158
ghee, 36, 88, 90, 101, 102, 163
ghormeh sabzi, 51, 109, 113
Ghormeh Sabzi ba Gharch, 108, 113
gifts, 49, 203
ginger, 32, 35, 65, 92, 219
goat cheese, 18, 68
gojeh sabz, 28
Gojeh sabz, 28
golpar, 35, 85, 189, 194, 195, 201, 203, 205, 206
Golpar, 35, 85
grains, 11, 38, 39, 160
Grains, 19
grape leaves, 143, 190, 191
Grape leaves, 29
grapes, 77, 110, 111
Green Bean Rice, 159, 171
grocery stores, 16, 18, 19, 20, 26, 27, 29, 31, 35, 37, 42, 82, 214
ground beef, 17, 28, 130, 131, 141, 143, 147, 156, 171, 190, 192
ground lamb, 126, 173, 196
guest, 5, 6
guests. *See* Guest

H

haleem, 21, 56
Haleem, 54, 56
halibut, 140, 150
ham, 71, 158
heart, 10, 17
Herb and Kidney Bean Stew with Mushrooms, 108, 113
herbal, 13, 34
herbs, 11, 15, 17, 22, 24, 29, 31, 39, 42, 47, 51, 55, 69, 78, 80, 83, 85, 86, 87, 91, 95, 98, 106, 109, 111, 113, 115, 116, 119, 120, 125, 127, 128, 129, 130, 131, 132, 134, 140, 141, 142, 144, 146, 156, 159, 166, 167, 169, 170, 172, 174, 176, 177, 183, 194, 195, 202, 203, 206
hoagie, 149
honey, 13, 55, 59, 60, 62, 68, 72, 78, 150, 151, 154, 208, 211, 212, 217, 218, 223, 225, 228
Honey, 54, 55, 68, 209, 217, 218, 225
Honey-Almond Brittle, 209, 218
honeydew, 233
Honeydew and Mint Smoothie, 227, 233
hospitality, 5, 6, 9, 49
Hot sauce, 156

I

ice cream, 214, 219, 222
infuser, 40
Ingredients, 7, 16
Iran, 1, 3, 4, 10, 11, 12, 15, 17, 18, 20, 21, 22, 26, 27, 31, 33, 35, 37, 70, 97, 149, 159, 194, 202, 209, 210, 222, 226, 228, 231

Iranian-Style Pizza, 138, 154
Isfahan, 3

J

jalapeño, 203
Jasmine flowers, 229
Joojeh, 123, 124, 128

K

kabob maytabeh, 39, 44
Kabob swords, 39
Kabobs, 7, 17, 123, 124, 125, 126, 128, 129, 130, 132, 133, 134
Kalam Polow, 159, 173
kale, 75, 107, 199
kaleh pacheh, 17
Kashan, 3
kashk, 19, 67, 83, 156, 193, 195
Kashk, 19, 82, 182, 193
Kashk-e Bademjan, 182, 193
kettle, 40, 43, 215, 229
khoresht, 15, 39, 41, 42, 108, 109, 121, 160, 162, 166, 167, 170, 177
Khoresht, 7, 108, 109, 110, 112, 115
Khoresht-e Bademjan, 108, 110
Khoresht-e Gheymeh, 108, 112
Khoresht-e Karafs, 108, 115
kidneys, 17
kielbasa, 149
kiss on both cheeks, 49
Koobideh, 123, 124, 126
Koofteh Berenji, 138, 141
kotlet, 44
Kotlet, 182, 192
Kuku, 7, 97, 98, 99, 101, 102, 104, 105, 106, 107
Kuku Bademjan, 97, 102
Kuku Kadoo, 97, 101
Kuku Sabzi, 97, 98
Kuku Sib Zamini, 97, 99

L

Lamb, 16, 81, 84, 87, 108, 118, 123, 138, 139, 159, 168, 173, 182, 196
Lamb and Barley Soup, 81, 84

lamb shank, 84
lamb shanks, 139, 168, *See* lamb shank
Lamb, Apricot and Apple Stew, 108, 118
Lamb, Potato and Bean Soup, 81, 87
lavash, 20, 65, 66, 125, 127, 129, 163, 183
Lavashak, 209, 210
legumes, 11, 24, 35, 52, 108
Legumes, 23, 45
lemon, 17, 32, 40, 44, 65, 66, 70, 71, 73, 74, 75, 80, 95, 118, 121, 132, 140, 141, 142, 178, 187, 189, 190, 191, 210, 215, 223, 225, 232, 234
Lemon, 215
Lentil and Egg Breakfast Burritos, 54, 61
Lentil Rice, 61, 159, 170
Lentil Salad, 69, 74
Lentil Soup, 81, 85
lentils, 23, 45, 74, 82, 83, 85, 90, 110, 170
Lentils, 23
Lima beans, 24
lime, 34, 40, 44, 65, 66, 84, 110, 111, 112, 114, 121, 128, 129, 133, 134, 135, 157, 171, 198, 201, 203, 215, 230, 233
Lime, 13, 123, 128, 156, 182, 198, 209, 215
lime juice, 34, 65, 66, 84, 111, 114, 121, 128, 129, 133, 134, 135, 171, 198, 215, 230, 233
lime powder, 34, 203
limes, 28, 34, 87, 112, 113, 114, 115, 116
limoo amani, 34, 87, 112, 113, 115
liver, 17
Loobia Pokhteh, 182, 189
Low-Carb Cauliflower "Rice", 159, 181

M

Maash Polow, 159, 177
Maast o Khiar, 182, 185
Maast o Musir, 182, 188
Macaroni, 138
mahi, 18, 150
Mahi, 138, 140
Mahicheh, 138, 139, 168
mango, 133
marinades, 18, 33, 36, 44
marmalade, 55
mascarpone cheese, 225
mayonnaise, 71, 75, 135, 152, 153

Maytabeh, 123, 130
Meat, 13, 16, 126, 138, 141, 147
Medjool, 25
Metal skewers, 39
milk, 56, 57, 63, 96, 217, 235
Milky Rice Pudding, 209, 217
Minced Lamb Pastries, 182, 196
mint, 13, 31, 70, 78, 82, 86, 95, 102, 106, 115, 119, 131, 137, 143, 156, 185, 187, 190, 193, 194, 196, 203, 205, 206, 233, 236
Mint, 183, 187, 227, 233, 236
Mirza Ghasemi, 138, 145
Mixed Herb Rice, 140, 159, 169
Mixed Vegetable Pickle, 202, 203
Miz-e Sobhaneh, 54, 55
mortadella, 154, 158
Mortar and pestle, 40
mozzarella cheese, 154
mung, 23, 45, 177
mung beans, 23
mushrooms, 90, 113, 114, 132, 152, 153
mustard, 32, 71, 72, 74, 75, 78, 152, 153
My Mom's Chicken Noodle Soup, 81, 94

N

Nan Berenji, 209, 213
nan o panir, 19, 22
Nargesi, 54, 58
New Year, 18, 21, 97, 98, 140, 169
nigella seeds, 20, 22, 135, 195, 203, 205, 206
Nigella seeds, 22
Noodle Soup with Beans and Herbs, 81, 82
noodles, 82, 83, 215
Nowruz, 18, 23, 140
nutmeg, 35, 219
nuts, 3, 11, 13, 21, 22, 39, 73, 141, 159, 211, 212, 216
Nuts, 21, 47, 159, 165

O

oats, 56, 57, 62
Oats with Sweet Cinnamon Ground Turkey, 54, 56
Offal, 17

olive oil, 58, 61, 70, 71, 72, 73, 74, 75, 76, 78, 80, 95, 105, 106, 107, 120, 128, 129, 132, 133, 134, 135, 140, 145, 154, 158, 168, 171, 178, 179, 186, 187, 189, 194, 199, 201
Olive oil, 36, 158
Olives, 182, 183, 194
omelet, 13, 58, 195
onion powder, 134, 154
Onion, Egg and Fenugreek Soup, 81, 88
onions, 13, 22, 28, 39, 40, 42, 43, 44, 65, 66, 69, 82, 87, 88, 94, 99, 106, 109, 110, 116, 131, 132, 190, 193, 203, 205
Onions, 28, 42, 54, 65, 183, 202, 205
orange, 25, 37, 40, 63, 77, 119, 135, 143, 165, 226, 230
Orange Clove Almond Cookies, 209, 226
orange zest, 63, 165
oregano, 31, 74, 85, 101, 147, 148, 154
organ meats, 17, 152
orzo, 90, 91

P

Pantry, 7, 16, 35
paprika, 71, 134, 195
parboiling, 38
Parboiling, 44
parsley, 51, 67, 74, 80, 82, 95, 96, 98, 102, 106, 113, 115, 135, 140, 141, 143, 147, 148, 154, 169, 190, 203, 206
Parsley, 13, 31, 183
pasta, 75, 90, 94, 109, 147, 148, 178
pastry dough, 225
peaches, 11, 13, 59, 76, 133, 210, 225
peas, 23, 45, 71, 142, 147, 180
pepper, 58, 65, 66, 67, 70, 71, 72, 73, 74, 75, 76, 78, 80, 82, 83, 84, 85, 86, 87, 88, 90, 92, 94, 95, 96, 98, 99, 101, 102, 104, 105, 106, 107, 110, 112, 113, 114, 115, 116, 117, 118, 119, 120, 121, 126, 128, 129, 130, 131, 132, 134, 135, 139, 140, 141, 143, 144, 145, 147, 148, 149, 150, 151, 152, 153, 154, 156, 171, 173, 175, 178, 179, 180, 181, 185, 186, 187, 188, 189, 190, 192, 193, 194, 195, 196, 199, 201
Persian Fresh Fruit Salad, 69, 77

Persian Fried Rice, 159, 180
Persian Gulf, 12, 18
Persian limes, 28
Persian-Inspired Nachos, 138, 156
Persian-Style Spaghetti with Meat Sauce, 138
persimmon, 223, 224
Persimmon Cheesecake with a Chocolate Crust, 209, 223
persimmons, 25, 223
Persimmons, 25
Phrases, 50
Piaz dagh, 42
Pickled Eggplant, 202, 206
Pickled Garlic, 202, 208
pickled vegetables, 15, 22, 37, 158
pickles, 13, 35, 37, 71, 87, 127, 128, 129, 130, 132, 134, 202, 203
Pickles, 7, 37, 125, 202
pie crusts, 121
pineapple, 133
pistachios, 11, 21, 62, 73, 78, 165, 211, 214, 216, 219
Pistachios, 21
pizza dough, 154
Plum and Beet Salad with Sumac Vinaigrette, 69, 72
plums, 11, 28, 30, 72, 133, 210
pomegranate, 13, 24, 35, 36, 44, 46, 62, 78, 117, 135, 179, 194, 201, 230
pomegranate concentrate, 36
Pomegranate Marinated Flank Steak and Herb Salad, 69, 78
Pomegranate Salsa, 135, 136, 137, 156, 182, 201
Pomegranate Spritzer, 227, 230
Pomegranate syrup, 36
Pomegranate-Citrus Grilled Shrimp Tacos, 123, 135
Pomegranate-Nut Granola, 54, 62
pomegranates, 5, 10, 11, 24, 201
porridge, 21, 56
pot, 6, 38, 39, 45, 57, 66, 74, 82, 84, 85, 87, 88, 90, 91, 92, 94, 95, 96, 110, 112, 113, 114, 115, 116, 117, 118, 119, 120, 121, 139, 142, 143, 144, 147, 148, 152, 160, 161, 162, 163, 167, 168, 169, 170, 172, 174, 175, 176, 177, 178, 179, 180, 189, 210, 215, 216, 217, 229
potato, 29, 30, 44, 87, 99, 104, 112, 149, 163, 192, 193
potatoes, 35, 40, 71, 87, 96, 112, 143, 192, 195
Potatoes, 30, 182, 195
Poultry, 16, 17
pressure cooker, 45
Pulses, 45
pumpkin, 22, 30, 93, 179, 219
Pumpkin seeds, 92

Q

Quick and Easy Saffron-Rose Ice Cream, 209, 214
Quince, 27
quinoa, 80, 199

R

radishes, 6, 13, 29, 69, 135
Radishes, 29, 183
raisins, 62, 73, 74, 86, 170, 178, 180, 185, 217, 229
Raisins, 217
red beets, 72
red hot peppers, 206
red onion, 70, 72, 73, 74, 75, 76, 78, 131, 195, 201
red pepper flakes, 150, 151
reshteh, 82
rice, 5, 10, 11, 13, 15, 17, 18, 19, 21, 22, 23, 24, 26, 27, 30, 33, 38, 44, 51, 61, 85, 90, 108, 109, 111, 112, 114, 116, 117, 118, 119, 120, 125, 127, 128, 129, 130, 132, 134, 137, 139, 141, 142, 143, 144, 147, 151, 159, 160, 161, 162, 163, 164, 165, 166, 167, 168, 169, 170, 171, 172, 174, 175, 176, 177, 178, 179, 180, 181, 190, 213, 215, 216, 217, 225
Rice Flour Cardamom Cookies, 209, 213
Rice servers, 41
Roasted Carrot and Turnip Soup, 81
rolls, 149, 152, 153, 220
Rose Lemonade, 227, 232

rose petals, 35, 37, 59, 60, 64, 86, 93, 185, 221, 225, 234
Rose petals, 220
Roses, 34
rosewater, 10, 13, 34, 37, 63, 209, 211, 214, 215, 216, 217, 218, 220, 221, 228, 232, 234
Rosewater, 37, 209, 215

S

sabzi khordan, 31, 183
Sabzi Khordan, 182, 183
sabzi polow, 18
Sabzi Polow, 159, 169
saffron, 5, 10, 11, 13, 32, 40, 45, 52, 82, 83, 92, 95, 96, 99, 102, 115, 116, 118, 121, 124, 126, 127, 128, 129, 132, 133, 139, 143, 144, 159, 160, 161, 163, 165, 166, 167, 168, 169, 170, 171, 172, 173, 174, 175, 177, 178, 179, 180, 193, 209, 211, 214, 216, 218,219, 220
Saffron, 32, 45, 52, 81, 96, 123, 128, 159, 160, 163, 165, 167, 168, 169, 170, 171, 172, 173, 174, 177, 178, 179, 209, 214, 216
saffron water, 45, 52, 82, 83, 92, 95, 96, 99, 102, 115, 116, 118, 121, 126, 127, 128, 129, 132, 133, 139, 143, 144, 160, 161, 163, 167, 168, 169, 170, 171, 172, 173, 174, 175, 177, 178, 179, 180, 193, 216
salad, 15, 33, 70, 71, 72, 73, 74, 75, 76, 77, 79, 111, 116, 119, 120, 127, 128, 129, 130, 132, 134, 137, 142, 144, 151, 156, 158, 166, 167, 170, 172, 174, 177
Salad Olivieh, 69
Salad Shirazi, 69, 70
Salads, 7, 31, 69
Salmon, 18
Salting Eggplant, 46
samanu, 21
samovar, 40
sandwiches, 17, 37, 87, 192
sangak, 20, 183
sardi, 14
sausage, 65, 66, 149
Sausage and Potato Sandwiches, 138, 149

Sauté, 39, 85, 95, 113, 115, 149, 165, 168, 173, 178
scallion, 74, 114, 140
scallions, 13, 69, 82, 83, 86, 90, 95, 98, 113, 135, 141, 143, 156, 169
Scallions, 183
seafood, 18
Seeds, 21, 22, 159, 179
Seer Torshi, 202, 208
seltzer, 230, 231, 236
sesame, 20, 35, 62, 75, 131
shallot, 29, 58, 80, 107, 150, 151, 170, 181, 188
shallots, 13, 29, 95, 181, 188
Shallots, 29, 182, 188
Sharbat-e Ab Limoo, 227, 232
Sharbat-e Albaloo, 227, 231
Sharbat-e Anar, 227, 230
Shir Berenj, 209, 217
Shir Moz, 227, 235
Shirin Polow, 159, 165
Shishlik, 124
shrimp, 33, 135, 136
side dishes, 18, 184
skillet, 39, 97, 117, 130
slow cooker, 39, 45, 109
Slow cooker, 39
sofreh, 15, 23, 55
Sohan Asal, 209, 218
Soltani, 124
Sosis Bandari, 138, 149
soup, 17, 39, 81, 82, 83, 84, 85, 86, 88, 90, 91, 92, 93, 94, 95, 96
Soup-e Jo, 81, 84
soups. *See* Soup
Soups, 7, 81
sour cherry, 13, 55, 222, 231, *See* Tart Cherry
Sour Cherry Spritzer, 227, 231
Sour Cherry Sundae, 209, 222
sour cream, 19, 93
southern, 12, 37, 149, 150
spaghetti, 82, 147, 148
sparkling water, 230, 231, 236
Spiced Carrot Ice Cream Float, 209, 219
spices, 3, 11, 17, 22, 35, 40, 66, 76, 85, 92, 110, 118, 202, 203, 219, 228
Spices and Seasonings, 32

spicy, 12, 65, 119, 131, 171, 226
spinach, 30, 51, 58, 82, 83, 186
Spinach, 30, 54, 58, 182, 186
split peas, 23, 90, 91, 112, 141, 142
spring mix, 78
Squash, 30, 92, 159, 179
Starches, 19
stew, 13, 30, 39, 51, 110, 111, 112, 113, 118, 120, 121, 150
Stew Entrees, 7, 108
stews, 5, 22, 23, 30, 33, 37, 39, 42, 108
stock, 42, 80, 88, 90, 92, 95, 96, 120, 141, 142
stone fruits, 210
strainer, 40, 87
strawberries, 77, 133
Stuffed Bell Peppers, 138, 143
Stuffed Grape Leaves, 182, 190
stuffed peppers, 143
sugar, 13, 26, 32, 45, 56, 59, 62, 63, 117, 118, 119, 133, 165, 166, 167, 190, 200, 211, 213, 215, 216, 217, 218, 220, 221, 225, 226, 228, 229, 230, 231, 232, 233
sumac, 11, 13, 33, 72, 80, 95, 125, 130, 131, 137, 189, 198
Sumac, 33, 69, 72
sweet, 13, 21, 23, 24, 25, 26, 27, 30, 31, 33, 36, 62, 72, 76, 104, 106, 112, 117, 119, 133, 152, 165, 178, 209, 215, 217, 219, 220, 222, 226, 228, 233, 234
Sweet Potato, 97, 104

T

taarof, 48
Taarof, 48
taftoon, 20, 183
Taftoon, 21
Tahchin, 159, 175
Tahdig, 159, 160, 162, 163
Tamarind, 37, 138, 150
Tamarind concentrate, 37
tamarind pulp, 150
tarragon, 13, 31, 72, 78, 86, 143, 190, 203, 205, 206
Tarragon, 183
tart, 10, 13, 26, 27, 33, 44, 59, 75, 77, 131, 167, 222, 225

tart cherries, 26
tart cherry, 26, 77
Tart Cherry Rice, 159, 167
tea, 2, 5, 6, 11, 32, 33, 36, 40, 43, 48, 55, 60, 68, 213, 218, 228, 229
Tea, 36, 43, 227, 228, 229
Teapot, 40
Tehran, 3, 4, 10, 154, 198
tenderloin, 17, 124, 129
Tenderloin, 123, 129
The Persian Kabob-urrito, 123, 137
The Persian Muffuletta, 138, 158
The Ultimate Kabob Burger, 123, 131
thyme, 74, 120, 154
tilapia, 150
Toasted Mung Bean Rice, 159, 177
tofu, 67, 134
tomato, 13, 28, 70, 85, 87, 94, 102, 103, 110, 111, 112, 125, 131, 141, 142, 143, 144, 145, 147, 148, 149, 154, 171, 173, 189, 190
Tomato paste, 36
tomatoes, 55, 70, 87, 110, 111, 120, 125, 131, 132, 145
tongue, 17, 32, 152, 153
Tongue Sandwiches, 138, 152
Tools, 7, 38
torshi, 13, 15, 37, 114, 119, 120, 149, 158, 176, 202, 204, 205, 206, 207, 208
Torshi Bademjan, 202, 206
Torshi Piaz, 202, 205
tortilla chips, 137, 156, 201
tortillas, 61, 135, 137
tradition, 4, 6, 9, 15
trout, 140
turkey, 17, 56, 57, 65, 66, 141, 143, 175
turmeric, 11, 13, 32, 35, 58, 67, 74, 82, 84, 85, 87, 88, 90, 92, 94, 98, 99, 101, 102, 105, 107, 110, 112, 113, 114, 115, 116, 118, 119, 120, 126, 130, 131, 135, 139, 141, 143, 144, 145, 147, 149, 150, 156, 170, 171, 173, 175, 177, 180, 187, 189, 192, 193, 195, 196, 203
Turmeric, 32

V

vanilla extract, 59, 220, 223, 225

vegetables, 17, 31, 39, 40, 42, 69, 71, 96, 132, 134, 143, 159, 175, 202, 203
Vegetables, 28
vegetarian, 52, 67, 97, 108, 113, 145, 170
verjuice, 13, 110, 111
vinegar, 65, 66, 72, 76, 78, 118, 173, 202, 203, 204, 205, 206, 208

W

Walnut, 55, 108, 117, 183
walnuts, 11, 47, 72, 86, 98, 117, 145, 146, 158, 185, 194
Walnuts, 22, 47, 182, 194
watermelon, 22, 26, 77, 133, *See* Watermelons
watermelons, 11
websites, 16
wheat, 11, 21, 56
Wheat, 21
whey, 19
White mulberries, 27
White Rice with Saffron (Chelow) and Crisp Golden Crust, 159

Y

yellow onion, 42, 67, 78, 82, 84, 85, 90, 92, 94, 96, 102, 106, 110, 112, 113, 115, 117, 118, 119, 120, 121, 126, 128, 129, 130, 131, 139, 141, 143, 147, 149, 152, 156, 171, 173, 175, 177, 180, 187, 189, 196, 199
Yellow split peas, 23
yellow squash, 30
yogurt, 5, 13, 14, 15, 18, 41, 44, 59, 60, 62, 71, 73, 85, 86, 87, 90, 91, 95, 111, 114, 116, 119, 120, 124, 127, 128, 129, 130, 131, 132, 134, 137, 141, 142, 144, 146, 163, 166, 167, 170, 172, 174, 175, 176, 177, 184, 185, 186, 187, 188, 195, 236
Yogurt, 18, 69, 73, 81, 86, 90, 95, 123, 125, 159, 175, 182, 184, 185, 186, 187, 188, 195, 227, 236
Yogurt with Cucumber, 182, 185
Yogurt with Eggplant, 182, 187
Yogurt with Spinach and Garlic, 182, 186
Yogurt, Mushroom and Split Pea Soup with Orzo, 81, 90

Z

Zeytoon Parvardeh, 182, 194
Zoroastrians, 97
zucchini, 30, 101, 132

About the Author

Tina Rezvani is a culture and food enthusiast and writer living in Atlanta, Georgia. She is passionate about educating others about our colorful and exciting world. She is a graduate of Georgia State University with a master's degree in cultural anthropology and of Emory University with bachelor's degrees in anthropology and comparative literature. Beyond writing, cooking, and eating, Tina loves the arts and spending time in nature.